A PEOPLE'S HISTORY OF CAPITALISM

TOM TORTORICH

Green Effect Media

Kansas City, MO
www.GreenEffectMedia.com

Green Effect Media

Contents

"The issue which has swept down the centuries and which will have to be fought sooner or later is The People vs. The Banks."

—*Lord Acton*
Historian, 1834

PART 1

A Brief History
of Capitalism

Everything You Know
About Capitalism Is Wrong

MOST of us are not Capitalists. We think that living in a Capitalist system makes us all Capitalists. But most of us misunderstand or have been intentionally misinformed or *un*educated about what Capitalism really is and who the Capitalists are.

Probably fully 95% of us, if not more, are not Capitalists. We're not rich enough to be. The word Capitalist simply refers to a member of the Capitalist Class.

Under a Capitalist regime, everything comes down to making money, to greed. That's the Golden Rule. Not, 'Do onto others' but 'Do onto oneself.'

If you're a wage-earner (or an unemployed wage earner) like the vast majority of us are, the career path you're on demands you work for a Capitalist and participate in a Capitalist system, but that doesn't make you a Capitalist.

Even being an entrepreneur doesn't necessarily have to make a Capitalist out of you. Many of the most successful entrepreneurs aren't. They might become Capitalists later, but they didn't start out that way. Steve Jobs (the late founder of Apple) started out in his basement without a penny to his name, only an idea that would change the world.

◇

IN THE HIERARCHICAL economic-centric society we have, known as Capitalism, the Capitalist Class are the aristocracy.

A Capitalist Class can emerge in *any* society, not just a Capitalist society.

Just as a Middle Class can emerge in any society, not just Capitalist society.

But in a Capitalist society, the Capitalist Class are the aristocrats.

In an Aristocracy, the Aristocratic Class are the Monarchs.

In a Monarchy, the Monarchs are the kings and queens.

In today's Capitalist society, the Capitalist Class sits at the top of the podium, below which are the Upper Class, the Middle Class, the Working Class, the Working Poor and the Lower Class.

Capitalists are a ruling class. No more, no less.

No, they're not political rulers. They're not necessarily interested in political office.

If you're a wage-earner, like most of us are,
you work for a Capitalist, you're participating
in a Capitalist system, but you're not a Capitalist.

Capitalism is not our form of political government in the United States. In the course of our education, this distinction is often blurred. It's a common misconception that the Constitution sets up a Capitalists State. No, it sets up a Republic (a form of government). Capitalism is not a State. It's a term that refers to the economy, not the government. Those two things should not be confused, or combined. The combination of Capitalism and State is as dangerous as the combination of Church and State.

The Golden Rule of Capitalism

UNDER the rule of the Capitalist Class, the rest of us—from the Upper Class on down—have been living manic, fast-paced lifestyles where we are defined by our things, live our jobs, and are slaves to debt.

We are perpetually unhappy. A mindset of greed has been cultivated, which makes us perpetually unsatisfied.

I don't think any good Capitalist would disagree with the notion that Capitalists are defined by greed. Ben Stein (more on him later) tells us greed is a fundamental part of human nature. Ayn Rand tells us selfishness is a virtue. Rand's philosophies were influential in the development of the currently in-favor Chicago school of economics.

Under today's Capitalist regime, everything comes down to making money, to greed. The Golden Rule of Capitalism seems to be 'Do onto oneself' not, 'Do onto others.'

◇

YET THE CAPITALIST Class in our society constitutes only about 5% of us. Or less.

There's the 1% who crashed the economy which they themselves created, and probably another 4% (or less) who are philanthropic Capitalists that give the rest of their class a good name.

And then there's the rest of us who are convinced we are all Capitalists, too.

We are taught in school that Capitalism has given us everything we have today. Look at all the wealth Capitalism created, the wealthy tell us.

Wealth allows us to send food to starving children in Africa.

The profit motive has given us the Industrial Revolution, the world's first true Middle Class, single-family homes that would be the envy of Kings and Emperors, electricity, telephones, automobiles, and iPads.

Let's leave aside for the moment that our things probably own us, and also leave aside the question of whether we were fundamentally happier before the industrial, electrical and technological revolutions. Poorer, yes, of course, this was a world without Capitalism. But happier.

Capitalism requires perpetual growth: A dollar
spent must mean at least three dollars earned.

Yes, the revolutions of the modern world grew out of a Capitalist society, sponsored by Capitalists with the sole desire to make a profit.

But there's no reason that a Middle Class, the industrial, electrical and technological revolutions couldn't have happened in the absence of Capitalism. And those revolutions might actually have been the better for it.

As it is, Capitalism has crippled us into being completely beholden, addicted,and subservient to technologies that otherwise would have been purely beneficial for the human race.

Conceived as the offspring of another system, they could have brought about utopia, not profit.

A PEOPLE'S HISTORY OF CAPITALISM

A Dollar Spent is ...
Three Dollars Earned?

WHY have we become slaves to our things?
Because Capitalism requires perpetual growth to continue its existence. Every dollar of capital invested has to make money in three (if not more) ways:

1) Pay back the original investor;
2) Profit the person or company who took out the loan;
3) Pay interest.

That's a very hard-working dollar.

And that's why Capitalism requires perpetual growth: a dollar spent must mean at least three dollars earned.

A successful Capitalist business model isn't satisfied by fulfilling a need, or even by creating a need; it has to create an ongoing need.

◇

CAPITALISM IS NOT consumerism. A person can buy products, spend money and not be a Capitalist and not even live in a Capitalist society.

Consumer Capitalism is a society that's convinced (brainwashed) into believing it not only needs to buy stuff, but that it must buy more, better stuff all the time. Have the latest, greatest technology at its fingertips. Newer is always better.

This is an addiction cultivated by Capitalists, who are the only ones who really think they perpetually need *more and more and more.*

More things, more money, more productivity, more profit.
Always more.

It's a sickness. It's a treadmill that's particularly hard to get off. But we have to. And there are ways.

But before we discuss what those ways might be, let's take a step back and look at where the heck it all started from.

I bet the answer will surprise you.

Capitalism is a relatively new idea. While Western Civilization has existed for over six thousand years, Capitalism is less than 500 years old.

THE
Big Three

Trouble sires three children, bad things come in threes, and there is a triumvirate of dueling mentalities pre-eminent in the Western Mind that have been getting us into a whole mess of trouble for a rather long while. Not to be overly dramatic or cynical about the whole thing, but Western Thought seems to be a pandemic of mass hysteria that has by now infected nearly all of humanity.

The history of the past 6,500 years, since the very dawn of Western Culture has been based on the first two of those beliefs:

Anything Nature Can Do We Can Do Better

First, there was the Western Mind's belief that Man's destiny was to conquer the world. It's why we were put on this Earth. A booming voice from the sky told us so.

We have the right and in fact the *charge* to rule over every living creature that moves on the ground or flies in the air or swims in the sea. We've been working towards that self-fulfilling destiny ever since. And we have to succeed! We don't want to disappoint the booming voice.

Might means Right

This is what allows The West to rationalize the brutal force it uses in subjugating the entire world without any need for wasting precious time considering any pesky moral implications of any of its actions.

This is the belief that Man alone possesses superior might, superior intelligence, superior... well, superior superiority.

We believe we are separate from and unequaled in the world

around us, nothing at all like any of the other life forms around here, and a far cry from the Ape-like creatures we left in the evolutionary dust. Our intelligence, ingenuity, creativity and consciousness knows no rival.

And when we started believing Man was superior to everything else on Earth, it was only a matter of time before we decided that some men were superior to some other Men (and women).

◇

THE RISE OF Western Civilization began with those ideas, and, over the next 6,500 years, took us far, far way away from our simple lives as hunter-gatherers. After awhile, it took us right into the Dark Ages of Medieval Europe. There, Western Civilization stalled for 1,000 years.

> When our third great belief rose from the ashes
> of the Dark Ages, the triumvirate of Western
> Thought was complete.

By then we had tried to conquer the entire world several times, but failed. Our bid for dominion over everything resulted in the collapse of every Empire that ever existed.

Rome had been our last, best hope. It managed to conquer about 75% of the known Western world before it collapsed under its own weight.

And when the empire fell, it took the whole of the known Western world with it. The Western world plunged into 1,000 years of ignorance, Holy Wars, Feudalism and fear.

All progress we had made towards conquering the World and re-creating it in our own image was erased.

Western Civilization had hit a road block.

Economic Imperialism
The first two beliefs held by Western civilization exemplifies

our arrogance, conceit and contempt for everything not-us.

But despite our superiority complex, we were a wasp without a bite.

As it turned out, all of the known world Rome took down with it was something less than 10% of Earth.

We'd seen some pretty dark days of Western world history up to that point, but we were little more than a pesky little menace. We posed no real threat to the rest of the planet. Only to ourselves.

Our mindset was incomplete.

When our third great belief rose from the ashes of the Dark Ages, the triumvirate of Western Thought became complete.

The first two beliefs were responsible for the first 6,500 years of the Western world. The idea that has been the driving force and obsession of the Western World for the past 500 years is that economic imperialism will conquer the world.

A Brief History
of the Western World

THE Three Beliefs —

Belief One is what we're trying to do.
1) We are destined to conquer the world;

Belief Two gives us license to do it.
2) Might means right;

Belief Three gives us the means to succeed.
3) Economic Imperialism will conquer the world.

These equally dangerous, equally false beliefs are responsible for the rise of a very small group of humans who felt justified in subjugating the entire world under the shackles of Western Thought.

◇

THE WEST'S FIRST Great Empire rose in a land called Sumeria about 6,500 years ago.

It conquered a relatively small region today known as the Near East before it collapsed a few thousand years into its reign.

Modern history is a merely a microcosm of the whole history of Western Civilization.

Then Western thought migrated to Africa, giving rise to a civilization that expanded to conquer the Sahara .

East of Egypt, a young kid named Alexander later founded his

A PEOPLE'S HISTORY OF CAPITALISM

own Empire—a remarkable feat for someone so young. But then again, at the time, Western civilization was still young, too.

It still is, really. Childlike.

Eventually, all great civilizations have fallen when the three beliefs infected another group of people who started enacting them more ruthlessly than the last.

> Our punishment for not teaching history is that we
> don't learn from it. And the punishment for not
> learning from it is repeating it.

And so it happened that the three beliefs migrated to a small peninsula shaped like a boot, which conquered more of the world than almost all its imperial predecessors combined. Western Civilization was getting a little too good at this game.

But the Empire in the boot also collapsed under its own weight when mightier, rightier people got sick of the mighty, righty Rome.

After the ensuing 1,000 years of ignorance and fear, a blip in the "progress" of Western Civilization, we can now take up the narrative of Modern History.

◇

MODERN HISTORY, THE history we are mainly taught in school, is a microcosm of the entire story of Western Civilization. We don't even teach our next generation most of that story. And our punishment for not teaching history is that we don't learn from it. And the punishment for not learning from it is repeating it.

And we have been. For 6,500 years.

The two beliefs made their way to the far west side of the know Western world called Europe, where Empires of various nationalities arose and all thought they should be the ones to conquer the world.

One Empire finally rose above the rest, called the English Empire.

Now in the course of human events, English folk found themselves best able to enact our so-called play.

Why? As it happened, their little island was mostly covered with forest. But they didn't think of it as forest, they saw only timber which they used for building the world's largest fleet of naval ships.

And with those ships, England built a great Navy (a Latin word meaning ship) whose superior might allowed them to dominate the economy of world trade. This was the first Empire to have the third belief, the superiority of economics, in its arsenal.

◇

IT EVENTUALLY CAME to be that the people of the island empire burned up or cut down most of their entire forest (it was a small island after all).

But they still had a few good ships. So they set sail in those ships to search for more wood to build even more ships. A stowaway on the voyage across the pond, the three beliefs were transmitted to the New World and started to flourish there, too.

Upstart colonials eventually got sick of the mighty, righty English.

Soon, descendents of the colonials who successfully rebelled started their own Empire and the whole process began all over again. David became Goliath.

◇

AND THUS IT came to be that in our time, in our particular link in the chain we find ourselves shackled by, there came from a very small strand of latitude on Earth, a group of humans who are merely the youngest in a long lineage of humans who think they're better than everybody else.

It's always a small group who thinks that way. Proving that fact, today's group possesses the genetic mutation for an almost complete lack of pigmentation in their skin.

A PEOPLE'S HISTORY OF CAPITALISM

While an organism with complete absence of melanin is called an albino, an organism with a significantly diminished amount of melanin is described as *albinoid*. Compared with the rest of the human race, that's today's Powers that Be. This is an evolutionary disadvantage, making this "elite" group ill-suited to live anywhere in the rest of the world except their native motherland of rainy skies and gales.

The American economic and military empire in its modern form is merely an extension of the once great British Empire.

We speak the same language

We believe in the same God.

Our political leaders are the same W.A.S.Ps (White Anglo Saxon Protestants.)

Our economic elite are the Capitalist Class.

In the history books written in the future, the chapter discussing today's civilization will be entitled, *The Royalist and United Corporations of America and England in the Age of Imperialist Capitalism.*

It will tell how a small group of people succeeded where Rome had failed, where Alexander the Great fell short, where Egypt ended. It will tell of The Great Global Empire that came to re-create the world in its own image.

If today's pestilence of mass hysteria doesn't break soon,
our global civilization will be swallowed in the
Great Flood of Western Thought.

And of how this civilization did that by convincing the World to follow it into temptation (of materialism and greed).

And how they did so without remorse.

And how, I wonder, will this Chapter in the history books of the future end?

And what chapter will follow?

The Firſt Bailout

SUMER, Rome, Egypt, and all the other ancient civilizations were all military empires. That is, they conquered the world with their military muscle. They exemplified the belief that might meant right.

But history reached a crucial turning point when the belief that *might meant right* took a back seat to the idea that *economic superiority means right.*

The First World Empire founded as a commercial venture was The British East India Company (1600-1873).

Though maintaining a militia had always been the sole trust of the State, The East India Company encountered so much foreign resistance (and competitors) that it decided to raise its own army.

And that's a scary thought. A well-equipped, well-trained army under the command of a corporate CEO.

But that's what the East India Company did, and did it well.

The Battle of Plassey was a decisive campaign for British East India Company. Their victory established the world's first Corporate Colony on the Indian Subcontinent.

And that was only the beginning. The East India Company eventually became ruler of territories vastly larger than the United Kingdom itself.

The East India Company truly was the world's first Corporate Empire.

And thus began an epic power struggle that continues to this day between Corporation and State.

Empires under State control are called Monarchies.

Empires under Corporate control are called Monopolies.

WHEN THE EAST India Company found itself close to bank-ruptcy in 1773, it went to the British crown for a bailout.

Evidently, it was discovering that wars are expensive. (Egypt, Rome or even the British could have told them that.)

A military is even more problematic for a for-profit corporation because it represents a huge cost that cuts into the would-be profits of the shareholders, whom Corporations are beholden to.

The British Crown agreed to bailout the East India Company.

The terms of the government bailout were that two members of the company's board of directors would be selected from members of the British Cabinet.

The merger of corporate and state interests usually means ignoring what's in the best interest of the people.

Previously, shareholders' meetings had made all decisions about the colonies in the India and the East. Now shareholders and elected officials would share in making decisions about the Imperialist colonies.

The Age of Economic Imperialism had dawned.

◇

MODERN ECONOMIC THOUGHT would never allow a corporation to control an army. The shareholders would never stand for it. *You're going to cut into our profits by doing what?*

Yet today there are many corporate interests that would require military support.

In centuries to come, Corporations would begin to take a different tact to maintain their own armies. They would attempt to exercise control over the State itself. If successful, this strategy would effectively allow a corporation to have carte blanche control of an army without cutting into profits. Armies could be used to fight corporate wars to benefit the shareholders, but financed by state-collected tax dollars.

The problem being, of course, that those taxes, collected from the people are then used against the best interests of the people.

Tax dollars should be used to maintain *the commons*, things like running water, sewage, better roads, bridges, all the infrastructure necessary that makes civilization possible.

This corporate plan of socializing costs (the expense of the army) at the expense of the People while privatizing the profits is a key component to fascism—the merger of corporate and state interests. (Which usually means ignoring the people's interests).

This corporate-military concept is exactly what we're seeing in today's Oil Wars. These are not wars of the State, these are Corporate wars for control over the world's oil supply.

And the roots of all this date back to the Battle of Plassey in 1757 and the Crown's bailout of the East India Company in 1773.

A Capitalist's History
of the United States

THE American Revolution was one of the world's first Corporate Wars—ignited by revolt against Capitalist practices.

The question of Imperialist control over commerce (of tea and tobacco and other goods), in large part, wasn't political. It was economic. The issue at hand was a variation of what we today call "free trade." Known as the Tobacco War among Southern Farmers, the American Revolution did not start out as a revolution. It was a trade war, and far more economic than political.

Today we miss the distinction between economic policies and political policies.

Today we confuse, misunderstand or are simply ignorant of the distinction between economic policies and political ones. Economics has so infiltrated and corrupted the realm of government that many distinctions have become muddled. But there *is* a clear divide.

Part of our confusion is directly related to the way history is taught—including the history of our own American Revolution, which gives us the image of a political rebellion.

Today we hear about a "minimum wage." But have you ever hear of "maximum wage" laws? Maximum wage laws were one of the issues at stake in the war America grew out of.

Maximum wages are not a cap on how much CEOs can make. (There should be laws like that.) Rather, maximum wage laws set a maximum, not a minimum, wage that corporations are legally allowed to pay unskilled laborers.

The truth is, the American Revolution wasn't even so much against the idea of corporate control, or even necessarily against free-trade policies. It was against the idea that the interests of the British Monarchy and The East India Monopoly being placed in front of colonial interests. Those policies crippled a truly American economy from coming into its own.

It was economic sovereignty as much as political sovereignty we were after.

History books, I think, get the *facts* about history right some of the time, but the underlying motivations tend to reflect the historians, not the history.

Contagion

THE Economic Empire that grew out of America is one of the most dangerous the world has ever seen.

The United Corporations of America is currently enacting the three beliefs more ruthlessly than any empire that's come before it.

Each successive Western Empire has been more successful than the last, expanding further, conquering more, dominating a larger sphere of influence.

Today, for the first time, that sphere of influence is truly global.

Civilization has developed unprecedented technologies in order to assert our superiority. (You see, at the heart of it, we really suffer from an inferiority complex.) This time, it's not just one forest on one island that's under attack (as if that wasn't bad enough). It's all the forests everywhere.

It's not just one Corporation subjugating one part of the world (as if that wasn't bad enough). It's a thousand corporations. And the world isn't big enough for all of them.

And it's not just one Empire that will collapse this time. For the first time, today's global empire really might accomplish its mission of conquering *everything*.

All previous empires have collapsed. Dictatorships, Monarchies, Monopolies. Every one. And let's not forget what happened when the Roman Empire collapsed.

When it fell, it took the known world with it and plunged our civilization into 1,000 years of feudalism and fear.

◇

PATHOLOGICAL BEHAVIOR IS infectious.

It catches like wildfire.

Richard Dawkins calls it a "virus of the mind," or the word

he coined, a *meme*—like *gene*.

The beliefs we hold are like our civilization's DNA.

And all beliefs, no matter how helpful are harmful, like DNA, are self-replicating. Or, like viruses, highly contagious.

You might even say that a pathological belief—like *might makes right*—is like a cancer or the black plague.

When enough people do or believe something, no matter how moral, immoral, or bizarre, that behavior becomes acceptable.

When everyone's doing it, that behavior becomes normal.

When everyone's behaved a certain way for a long enough time, we forget that there ever was any other way.

It's only afterwards, perhaps not until we read about ourselves in history books, that we shake our heads and wonder, what the heck came over us?

Why did we think blood-letting cured diseases? Why did we think the World was flat? Why did we believe in Zeus?

If today's pestilence of mass hysteria doesn't break soon, our global civilization will be swallowed in the Great Flood of Western Thought.

I do hope this isn't how our chapter of history ends. Though I fear it will be.

But however it ends, the transition will come soon.

Our modern way of life is completely unsustainable.

The Love of Money
Is the Root of All....

FIFTY years from now, perhaps only twenty-five, our world will be unrecognizable. It will either be filled with wonders beyond the wildest dreams of Star Trek, or succumb to humanity's wildest dreams of avarice and be plunged back into the Dark Ages. We've been approaching the precipice for the past century and a half, since the very birth of the idea of economic imperialism.

Alfred Marshall's book *Principles of Economics* brought the ideas of supply and demand, marginal utility and costs of production into a coherent whole. (If these terms are gobbledegook to you, that's good. It means you're not an economist and there's still hope for you.)

That cohesive whole which Marshall described quickly ascended to the sole *raison d'être*, the motivation behind all of Western Civilization's achievements ever since.

But Alfred Marhsall isn't to blame for the birth of modern economics. His book merely elucidated the subtext behind the prevailing cultural mindset of the era. It's what the East India Company had been practicing and which led to the Battle of Plassey in 1757.

Had Alfred Marhsall's theories not already been in ascendency, their conception would not have found expression through his pen, nor would his manuscript have met such widespread acclaim by the Powers that Were.

Thus it came to be that the single most destructive ideology solidified the Western World behind the green banner of economics.

Economic imperialism can be defined as: The belief that economics is the underpinning upon which all fundamental components of civilization should be based. This includes: government, laws, family, tastes, sociology, culture, religion, war, science, research, art, irrational behavior, rational behavior, politics, law and crime.

◇

FROM THE PEOPLE'S perspective—the people being the participants in civilization without whom the whole thing wouldn't be possible—the holy grail of civilization, the reason we participate, has been the quest to achieve utopia—either on Earth or in Heaven. Utopia is the reward for playing by the rules.

From our rulers' perspective, the whole point has been to conquer the world. But after trying and failing so many times, that idea was kind of getting a bit stale.

That's why we were meandering so aimlessly for a thousand years and a thousand nights in the middle ages. We finally warded off our cultural bout of depression round about the 14th century after some good old fashioned violent warfare known as the crusades.

Well, we figured, we're still a bit exhausted from trying to conquer the world, but now that the Crusades reminded us how good it made us feel to try, we figured we'd get ourselves back in the game.

So we did.

Then, alas, after long millennia of toiling in the dark, some really bright guys in the 19th century finally believed they had actually discovered the source of the spring from which all civilization flowed.

See, it was more than just a need to conquer the world. We needed to know *why* we wanted to conquer the world? What was the *point* in putting up with all that frustration? All our failures?

The discovery of what Jean-Paul Sartre would have called the *Ah-hah!* principle (of civilization as a whole!) finally came along.

And the *Ah-hah!* principle was .... *greed!* That was the reason behind everything! The whole struggle was for a much nobler purpose, and that nobler purpose was *Economic Imperialism*—we didn't only want to conquer the world, we wanted to conquer the world so that we could have all the money in the world!

The pursuit of greed!

Ah-ha!

Radix civilzation est cupiditas!

(The love of money is the root of civilization.) Just a small error in translation from the original Biblical quotation, *"Radix malorum est cupiditas."*

Myself, I personally would have thought, "Crap! All this time we've been doing all this nonsense just out of sheer greed?! What a waste of 6,500 years!"

But no, of course not. All the people who had been wasting the last 6,500 years for the rest of us got all excited about the whole thing all over again.

Now they could finally put a finger on exactly why it was they kept beating their heads against the wall, and that really helped put some wind back in their sails.

Greed is good!

Do you believe that's true? I certainly don't.

As it turns out, this theory is accepted only by Imperialists, and Capitalists, who, ironically, have used that very belief to convince the rest of us that they are the ones who should, and by right ought to be today's Masters of the Universe.

Ironically, the yellow brick road we've been following for these past few centuries does not lead to the promised utopia, but towards the ultimate dystopia.

Ben Stein's Greed

THERE is no clearer indictment that the destructive and tyrannical ideology of *Greed is Good* is in fact the preeminent belief held by Powers that Be than right-wing economist Ben Stein.

In 2011, Stein served up on a silver platter an op-ed in the Wall Street Journal which is as much a confession as it is an opinion.

His piece was addressed to the contemporary Occupy Wall Street movement, which Stein accurately characterized as being against greed.

Stein proceeded to take up his sword and shield (and pen) to defend greed against the tyranny of the liberals.

Quoth the economist:

Greed is a basic part of animal nature. Being against greed is like being against breathing or eating....

And what does it mean to be against corporations? Corporate ownership is by far the most efficient, responsible way of organizing industrial production there has ever been.

Ben Stein's notion that greed is a fundamental part of human nature is absolutely absurd. It's a fundamental part of Capitalist nature, but not human nature.

Proponents of economic imperialism like this should (and I believe will in some utopian future) be charged and convicted by our descendents of crimes against humanity and sentenced to some kind of Capitalist Punishment.

The punishment should fit the crime, so now we have to go about the work of exploring just exactly what those crimes are before we can move on to sentencing.

A PEOPLE'S HISTORY OF CAPITALISM

THE ORIGINS OF THE MIDDLE CLASS

A MIDDLE Class is actually a very rare thing in the history of civilization. Only the most "successful" civilizations ever achieve one. Most civilizations consist of oppressors and the oppressed, with almost no one anywhere in the middle.

That way of life climaxed in the West during the 1,000 year reign of feudalism in the Dark Ages.

There were many factors that caused the transition away from feudalism and into Capitalism.

The Black Plague was the death blow for feudal society.

In some countries, as many as 1 in 2 Europeans died in the space of 4 years (1346-1350).

As you can imagine, a population decline of such an unprecedented proportions decimated the existing social and political landscape.

In many ways, it was back to the drawing board.

The ideas of the European Renaissance had already been planted, and they would blossom on this new, blank slate.

Suddenly—in the space of a single generation—all the rules that had been in effect for the past 1,000 years were thrown out the window.

◇

ONE CAN ONLY wonder if anyone alive at the time truly realized their way of life was inexorably headed towards collapse.

Was anyone considering, "Hmmm, our conditions are very unsanitary. There's more peasants than nobles. This way of life just doesn't seem sustainable."

If there had been a printing press at the time, would anyone have written a book called, *Tear Down Feudalism?*

THE IDEAS OF the European Renaissance included social, political and economic transformations, and an intellectual revitalization of Western Europe with strong philosophical and scientific roots. This was not the same movement as the Italian Renaissance (a literary and artistic movement a few centuries later,) although one good Renaissance deserves another.

The ideas of the European Renaissance arrived from the East, brought back by the Crusades Europe had waged for control of Jerusalem in the East.

There, over the past 1,000 years, the ancient knowledge the West had accumulated before the fall of Rome had been preserved.

IN THE BRAVE New Europe after the Black Death of Feudalism, a passion for new ideas and new things (largely from the East) swept over the land.

A new merchant class began to arise. Our society still remained hierarchical, with the nobility (upper class) owning the countryside, and the peasantry (lower class) working the countryside, but now something new started happening. A new bourgeoisie class (literally "town-dwellers") started to arise in the cities. They would come to make a very good living through trade. They were merchants, peddlers of all things East.

They would evolve into the new Middle Class.

One definition of 'Middle Class' equates this class with the original meaning of Capitalist: *someone with so much capital that they could rival nobles.*

THE ORIGINS
OF CAPITALISM

HE rise of the Middle Class and the rise of Capitalism are inexorably linked.

Capitalists would have you believe their class gave rise to an affluent Middle Class, but that's like the chicken calling the egg a patsy.

The truth is, the chickens hatched from an affluent Middle Class, grew up to be Ponzies, and tied the yolk of Capitalism around the rest of us.

◇

TRADESMAN AND MERCHANTS sell goods to make money as a means to an end. That end being: feed your family, work for a better life.

But in Capitalism, the accumulation of wealth becomes an end unto itself. A Capitalist doesn't make a living by making products, or selling goods, but *makes a living off accumulated capital.*

It's the idea that rich people don't have to work. Their money can work for them.

But where did the accumulated capital come from? From the success of Middle Class merchants who became corrupted by greed.

The European Renaissance produced some fine things—the first Democratic Republics since Greece and Rome, the English Parliament, the printing press, and the origins of modern Universities—Capitalism was not one of them.

THIS ALL HAPPENED around the 13th and 14th centuries. So believe it or not, Capitalism has only been around for a relatively short time. Trouble is, a human lifespan is even shorter, and some of us have been playing this Capitalist game for so many generations that we can't remember any other way, or at least any *better* way.

SOME SUCCESSFUL MERCHANTS took it upon themselves to help other new, aspiring, or less-successful merchants succeed by lending them money (capital) out of their own pockets.

Credit was a revolutionary new idea. But why take that risk? And why concoct such a scheme in the first place?

Only in Capitalism is the accumulation of wealth an end unto itself.

If you believe it was to help your fellow man, I might say you're a dreamer.

Lenders did it to get paid back with interest, mostly motivated by greed.

Borrowers did it to expand their commerce, with the hope of making even more money in the long run. Some, no doubt borrowed out of greed. But for others, it was probably a risk they needed to take if they were to keep their businesses going and support their families.

IN THIS WAY, it was one small step for a successful merchant to transition out of the "merchant Middle Class" and into a "merchant Capitalist." But it was one giant leap (some would argue in the wrong direction) for the evolution of society.

A merchant and a Capitalist are not the same thing. A businessman or entrepreneur might earn his first million by building a successful business. It's only when that merchant takes his million and invests it in the fortunes of another man that a Capitalist is born.

So investors (lenders), not merchants (borrowers), were the first Capitalists.

Merchants had existed long before Capitalism.

◇

COMPANIES, BUSINESSMAN AND affluent societies can exist in the absence of Capitalism. Capitalism only emerges when the primary objective becomes making money for the investors, the shareholders, not making products or a better life for yourself.

Much of Western history for the past five hundred years is concerned with the development of Capitalism in its various forms.

While the idea of lending capital in the form of credit with the goal of getting back more than the principal was the first expression of Capitalism.

That practice isn't so bad, and certainly not all bad.

But just wait.

A whole new class of money men would step in pretty soon. Not bankers. They had already arrived on the scene.

Capitalists who made bad loans weren't going to just let that slide. Debt collectors came into existence. But that wasn't enough.

Enter the Brokers. These guys decided they could make money by selling insurance against unrecoverable bad loans.

Insurance was one of the first "financial products" ever invented, which started us down the road of Finance Capitalism.

Finance Capitalism has had a long history of corrupting Capitalism, turning it to the dark side of human nature.

A Perpetual Energy Machine

THE wheels of Capitalism were turning along just fine, making money for honest businessmen, semi-honest money lenders and unscrupulous finance Capitalists indiscriminately.

Prior to the dawn of the 18th century, all business and trade was based on human manpower. We could only trade (and make money on) what an army of laborers could produce.

But the hamster wheel of Capitalism, greased by greed, demands that the hamsters always run faster and faster and faster.

Every dollar of capital lent has to produce enough "new" money to satisfy the business owner, the investor, and the banks. That's a lot of hands in the till.

So there soon came a time when expansion of the "capital market" wasn't moving fast enough to keep all the greedy Capitalists satisfied. And so an army of restless Capitalists started a revolution.

It was known as the Industrial Revolution.

◇

THE INDUSTRIAL REVOLUTION was an aggregate of innovations, including the cotton mill, the steam engine, and the replacement of organic fuels based on wood with fossil fuel based on coal.

All of these things had a few things in common:

They all allowed for faster, more efficient, less labor-intensive production.

The machines were all quite elaborate contraptions that required a lot of investment capital to build in the first place. Without a whole fistful of dollars, an inventor might dream all day, but in this new era of Capitalism, without an investor in his pocket, nothing

32

would ever come of it.

The other thing that industrial innovations had in common is decreasing the cost of production. The more efficiently a machine converted energy to work, the more it nourished the growing beast of Capitalism.

Inventors even conceived the notion of a "perpetual energy machine," which would keep going and going and going with only one initial influx of "capital" a.k.a, energy. A perpetual energy machine would never stop.

But that was only a dream.

Or was it?

Successful Capitalism had manifested enough capital to manifest machines, which in turn manifested a huge burst in "productivity" which manifested even more capital.

Capitalism, itself, was seeming more and more like the very epitome of a perpetual energy machine.

Capitalism was on the rise towards dominating the modern Western World.

A Love Affair for the Ages

AMERICAN Economist Robert Emerson Lucas, Jr. said of the Industrial Revolution, "For the first time in history, the living standards of the masses of ordinary people have begun to undergo sustained growth ... Nothing remotely like this economic behavior has happened before."

Capitalists took most of the credit. Sure, they said, machines have revolutionized the world, but who would have ever invented them, or devised a way to use them if not for the profit motive?

The standard of living of the masses. That's the key. Without the masses for the tycoons to stand on the backs of, the whole thing would never have started, continued, or worked at all.

Capitalists always forget that. They need a Middle Class to stand on. Capitalism can only function in a hierarchical society where there's enough people with enough buying power to grease the wheels. Remember the original definition of 'Middle Class': *a class with so much capital that they could rival nobles.*

So the first Capitalists had been born of the Middle Class. Now they were consuming the Middle Class. The old Middle Class of Capitalists had all turned into investors.

So "Middle Class" would come to have a new definition: a class with enough money to buy the goods produced by industry. The "lower class" or "working class" would provide the labor necessary to run the industrial machines.

In short, the machine of Capitalism is not a perpetual energy machine. It needs a continuous influx of money and labor to keep its wheels churning. It needs high *living standards of the masses of ordinary people. And an ever increasing population.*

◇

CIVILIZATION NEEDS *some* motivating factor to promote

its expansion. With the proper motivation, oh the places we'll go. The profit motive is only one possible incentive.

What about the pure motivation for improving ourselves?

What about the quest for knowledge?

What about advancing science for science's sake? Or the simple desire to achieve a better standard of living for all—achieve utopia.

These all can provide ample motivation for the unprecedented success of a society and the lives of all its people.

Of course Capitalists don't believe in any of these things any more than they believe in luck or Santa Clause.

Capitalists claim that the profit motive is the sole reason for the birth and continued success of the Industrial Revolution and the meteoric rise of civilization over the past 150 years.

It's true: the advancements of civilization since the Industrial Revolution truly have been unprecedented. Nothing like this had ever occurred in the entire 6,500 year history of Western Civilization—in fact in the whole 70,000 years modern humans have walked the Earth. That's not in dispute.

The machine of Capitalism is not a perpetual energy machine. It requires a continuous influx of new money to keep its wheels churning.

What is in dispute is the Capitalists' claim that this unprecedented advance and affluence never could have happened in the absence of the profit motive.

But I would argue that Capitalism has stunted the development of as many ideas as it has spurred.

Whenever two competing technologies went head-to-head, Capitalism always financed the one with the potential to make the most profit. Not necessarily the better technology.

A more efficient electric car as well as an engine that ran on ethanol (the *alternative* fuels of today) were both invented before the gasoline-powered internal combustion engine.

Nikola Tesla's concept of wireless electricity demonstrated more potential but less profit than Edison's version.

Civilization is based on economics, greed and the intrinsic desire to make a profit, Capitalists claim—and just look at the world around you. It's living proof.

The truth is that in our history, the rise Capitalism and the rise of industry are inexorably linked.

Capitalism has stunted the development
of as many ideas as it has spurred.

The lie is the unprecedented success of civilization since the rise of Capitalism implies that Capitalism is the very underpinning, the foundation on which civilization itself stands.

It's simply not true.

Success could have come about in other ways, through other motivations. The world could be very different than it is today in the absence of the profit motive.

It would be much more egalitarian, cleaner, less polluted were Capitalism not around to cherry pick technologies that make the most profit while passing over efficient, cleaner, alternatives.

But Capitalists are blinded by the profit motive. They can't see anything except dollar signs.

They were having a love affair with the Industrial Revolution. Profiteers were profiting beyond even their own wildest dreams of avarice.

And it was about to get even better for them. And much much worse for the rest of us.

The Model-T of Mass Production

IF the first industrial revolution was a fiery love affair, the second industrial revolution was a marriage made in heaven for Capitalists.

The second industrial revolution included the advent of the assembly line.

Enter Henry Ford. His factories *were* the Model T for mass assembly, a Capitalists' wet dream come true.

Industrial Tycoons were already mass producing small, simple things. Individual interchangeable parts could be mass produced, but no one had yet found an efficient way to mass produce complex things.

In the early 20th century, Henry Ford did. He mass produced not only all the parts for the his Model T, but mass-assembled the whole thing.

Ford transformed the Middle Class into the backbone of Capitalism: a consumer class.

One small step for Ford, one giant leap for Capitalism.

In addition to making complex things faster and faster, assembly-line production had another, more significant effect. The price of production plummeted. Items as complex as the Model T could, for the first time in history, be marketed to and afforded by the average Joe.

Ford marketed his Model-T to the Middle Class when the automobile had previously been a toy for the rich. It was a defining moment in the history of Capitalism.

Ford understood the implications of this so well that he decided to pay his employees double the current standard daily wage so they could afford the cars they were manufacturing.

Ford was banking on all those wages ending up back in his pocket when his workers bought the cars. Ford transformed the Middle Class into the backbone of Capitalism: the consumer class. Today's Capitalists, in large part, have turned their back on the Ford principle. They pay as little as possible, not as much as they can afford. Every last cent Capitalists can scrape off the floor goes to line the pockets of the shareholders.

A penny saved is better than a penny re-invested.

Today's Capitalists, in large part, have turned their back on the Ford principle. They pay as little as possible, not as much as they can afford.

That strategy—milking the consumers dry by paying less than a living wage—is ultimately self-defeating.

Whether they're paying a pittance to American workers or outsourcing jobs to China, India and the Philippines and paying in rupees and yen, if no one anywhere makes any money, who do Capitalists thinking is going to buy all that crap they make? It just doesn't add up. It's short-sighted. But then again, looking beyond quarterly statements never has been a Capitalists' strong suit.

Ford was most definitely a job creator.

Today's Capitalists are not.

A PEOPLE'S HISTORY OF CAPITALISM

A Brave New Factory

FORD'S understanding of the essential role the common man played in the success of Capitalist tycoons came from his upbringing as a dirt-poor farmer. But that insight only extended so far.

In addition to giving us a world of mass-produced complexity, Ford also gave us a world of tedious, mind-numbing, repetitive factory labor.

One of the darkest sides of Capitalism is that it transforms us into an army of wage-earners. If left unchecked, the transfer of wealth from the majority to the minority increases exponentially, and the options for the masses, called the proletariat, narrow.

More and more become locked into the life of working class serfs for the class of society ironically referred to as *job creators*.

Without the monopolistic iron fist of the *job creators*, we wouldn't be locked into a social prison that requires us to work for someone else.

Aldous Huxley's *Brave New World* satirizes the sterile world of mass production the Ford factory created.

Today's jobs, sterile cubicles, white walls, white noise, fluorescent light, and glowing computer screens make the Ford factories seem like highly overstimulating environments.

Huxley envisioned a dark future controlled by industry where the laborers are slaves with mind-numbing jobs that atrophy their minds, lulling them into a trance. They are then easily brainwashed and told to spend all their money on all the products they spend all day making. That book was written in 1932.

Less than a century later, we seem to have arrived.

IT'S WORSE THAN Huxley imagined.

Today's workers might sit in sterile cubicles, deprived of all sensory input save Musak, white walls, white noise, fluorescent light, and the glow of their computer screens for more hours than the sun shines every day. This almost makes that old Ford factory look like an highly overstimulating environment.

After work, we come home to box-shaped, factory-manufactured housing where we stare into talking boxes that tell us which products to buy more of and how the manufactures aren't meeting their quarterly projections because consumer confidence is low.

The final irony may be that the brainwashing is so pervasive that each generation born into this world realizes the situation less and less.

Some of them become tomorrow's Capitalist Class.

And we all become rats in a maze led around by these blind mice who see nothing but dollar signs.

The Best Bubble-Blower
On the Market

CAPITALISM always needs an influx of new wealth. From time to time, it comes up against barriers limiting its growth. Each time, the solutions to break down those walls become more and more imaginative.

The Industrial Revolution broke down the first wall. Assembly lines and mass production (the Second Industrial Revolution) broke down the next wall.

But even the organic growth created by the first and second Industrial Revolutions would still never be enough.

The transfer of wealth to the top of the pyramid is exceeding the production of new wealth—at least, new real wealth. In the "Industrialized World," the transfer of wealth from the bottom 99% to the to 1% is all but complete.

Much of the history of the past 500 years has centered around new and more aggressive ways to manufacture capital. The most detrimental of all has been inventing the modern stock market, Wall Street.

It's like we're playing a global game of Monopoly and we're all about to land on Boardwalk and get wiped out. Congratulations, the Capitalists are about to win.

This is the ultimate barrier to growth. Much of the history of the past half millennia has centered around new and more aggressive ways to manufacture capital, which is the only life support system for Capitalism.

Today we're rapidly approaching a point where there's no

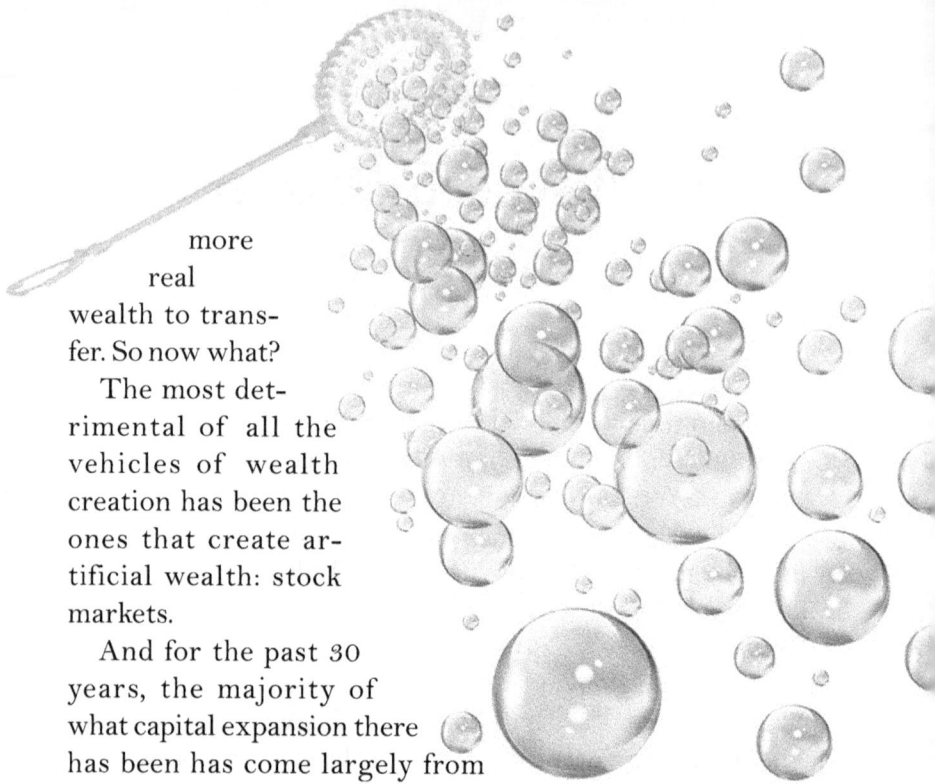

more
real
wealth to trans-
fer. So now what?

The most det-
rimental of all the
vehicles of wealth
creation has been the
ones that create ar-
tificial wealth: stock
markets.

And for the past 30
years, the majority of
what capital expansion there
has been has come largely from
blowing bubbles and manipulating markets.

While the first and second Industrial Revolutions provided organic growth, today we've turned almost exclusively to the stock market, looking for artificial growth. But whether real or artificial, perpetual growth cannot go on forever. It is not sustainable.

Wall Street is the best bubble-blower on the market.

The closer we come to the final wall, the faster and faster we accelerate towards it. We see it on the horizon. We've even given it a name: Wall Street.

Although stock exchanges have been around for more than 400 years, today's Wall Street is an absurd caricature of every stock market that's ever come before it. Wall Street is a Hail Mary pass with one second left on the clock of Capitalism. Wall

A PEOPLE'S HISTORY OF CAPITALISM

Street is the best bubble-blower on the market.

We're furiously huffing and puffing to keep the bubble
of all bubbles inflated—the money bubble
floating over Wall Street.

Derivatives, toxic mortgage-backed securities and all the rest are evidence of just how desperate is our last-ditch hope to keep Capitalism alive. We're furiously huffing and puffing to keep the bubble of all bubbles inflated—the money bubble floating over Wall Street.

And when Wall Street collapses, will it bring all of civilization down with it, or will a great roadblock on the path of human history finally be removed?

"A Santa Claus who prefers income redistribution [allows] Americans to work less and invest less, devoting more time to leisure.... "

—Jude Wanniski

(As if that were a bad thing.)

Taxes and a Two-Santa Theory
National Observer, 1976

PART 2

Economics
in
Wonderland

Drinking the Kool-Aid

The first official stock certificate was issued in 1606 for a Dutch company (*Vereinigte Oostindische Compaignie*) seeking to profit from the spice trade to India and the Far East.

Economic historians consider the Netherlands to be the first thoroughly Capitalist country. In Early modern Europe, it featured the wealthiest trading city (Amsterdam) and the first full-time stock exchange.

What economists term *the inventiveness* of the traders during this period led to insurance and retirement funds along with much less benign schemes such the one Isaac le Maire came up with. He forced prices down by dumping stock and then buying it all back at a discount—a strategy known today as a bear raid.

I don't call any of this inventive. The idea of *inventing* new ways to make money should not only be illegal, but certainly not encouraged and practiced by the upper echelon of society. But it us. And it's evidence of the mental illness of our civilization. There is even a little known law that makes it perfectly legal for any member of the United States Congress—and their staff—to engage in insider trading.

From insider trading to short selling, market manipulation is as old as the stock market itself, although granted, today's strategies have become significantly more complex.

And then there were bubbles.

The first was The Dutch Tulip bubble, which reached its height in 1636. Tulips—yes, the flower. A good Tulip trader could make 60,000 florins in a month, about $30,000.

Then one day in Haarlem a buyer failed to show up and pay for his tulip. The ensuing panic spread across Holland, and within days tulip bulbs were worth only a hundredth of their former prices. The tulip bubble popped quickly.

But we've been seeing financial bubbles ever since, growing out of a surge of irrational behavior, a desire to possess as much as possible of any given thing and a willingness to pay prices in excess of 1,000 times what that thing could ever possibly be worth. Charles Mackay, a 19th century writer, called this the principle of *extraordinary popular delusions and the madness of crowds.*

Also known as "Drinking the Kool-Aid."

In our system, money is mistaken for having intrinsic worth. Not based on value, not based on products, not based on anything.

Ultimately, the fantasy always ends, the bubble bursts, and everyone suddenly realizes the intrinsic worthlessness of the object of the bubble. Financial ruin ensues again and again and again.

◇

AS PERVASIVE AS this déjà vu has been, it wasn't until a new trend called disintermediation emerged that things really started to get scary.

At its core, disintermediation is the removal of intermediaries in a supply chain: "cutting out the middleman" so that more profits flow to the top.

When disintermediation was applied to Capitalism, something fundamentally new started happening.

Before Capitalism, money was a means to an end. (A better life.)

With Capitalism, making money became the end, and was achieved by selling products.

But some Capitalists started to realize how horribly inefficient that set-up seemed. (Inefficiency is the bane of Capitalists.)

Disintermediation would mean that money could be both the means and the end. Essentially, taking the *product* out of the middle.

Why make money making products, when Capitalists could make money making money in the stock market? If precious resources weren't wasted producing goods, that would mean extra capital to invest.

But wait, invest in what?

Fewer products means less wealth ... just more money. In this scenario, money becomes detached from value, from wealth, and literally becomes worth less than the paper it's printed on.

Hence the expression, *it takes money to make money* is more than just an axiom. It's the fundamental mindset responsible for the destruction of our civilization.

Disintermediation means eliminating the middle-man.
That's what the stock market does for money.
Why make money by making products when
you can make money making money?

In this system, money is mistaken for having intrinsic worth — not based on value, not based on products, not based on anything.

Just believed to be intrinsically valuable. It is not. By itself, it has no value.

And what does all this remind you of?

What happens when everyone believes something is worth 1,000 times its real value?

You get a bubble.

Money itself is today's financial bubble.

As absurd—arguably more so—than history's first bubble, where a single tulip was worth the price of a modern-day mansion.

This money bubble could be the bubble to end all bubbles.

It's bigger than anything we've ever seen.

What happens when it bursts?

So Dark the Con of E·con·omics

THE term "con-artist" is short for "confidence" artist. The person the con-artist is trying to deceive is known as the mark. If you're an accomplice to the con-man, you're called a shill.

A confidence artist is defined by Wikipedia as:

> Someone who attempts to defraud a person or group by gaining their confidence. He does so by understanding and exploiting characteristics of the human psyche such as greed, both dishonesty and honesty, vanity, compassion, credulity, irresponsibility, naivety, and the thought of trying to get something of value for nothing or for something far less valuable.

In a typical swindle, the con-man gives the mark his own confidence, encouraging the mark to in turn trust him. The con-artist thus poses as a trustworthy person seeking another trustworthy person.

> What do you call a con-man who tries to defraud another con-man? A stock broker.

The first known usage of the term "confidence man" in English was by the American press during the United States trial of William Thompson. Thompson's ruse was to chat with strangers until he asked if they had the confidence to lend him their watches. Then he walked off wearing it.

◇

CHANGE THE WORD from "con-man" to "stock broker" and the same definition applies almost verbatim—especially the part about trying to get something of value for something far less valuable.

The first two American stock-brokers who sold stock to each other standing on the corner of Wall St. and Broad St. in New York swapped their pieces of paper because each of them believed the other was getting the short end of the stick. At the same time, each man's game was to not let on to the other man that he thought the company who's stock he held was worth less. (read: worthless.)

So each man was playing the part of a con-artist.

And what do you call a con-man who tries to defraud another con-man? A stock broker.

Neither would have sold their piece of paper for the other piece of paper if they felt they already owned the more valuable piece of paper.

A trader will only sell a stock when he believes the value will keep going down. In order to sell, he must find someone to pay a price he himself believes is too high. Thus, trying to get something of value (money) for something far less valuable (the stock).

The trader on the other side of the bargain, too, only buys because he believes he's getting something of value (the stock) for something far less valuable (money).

They are both con-men.

◇

THIS BEHAVIOR IS the foundation behind the working model called Game Theory that economists use to describe and explain behaviors observed in the seemingly schizophrenic stock market.

This principle was originally worked out by mathematician John Nash. The 2001 movie *A Beautiful Mind* is the biography of John Nash and his life-long struggle with mental illness.

This mathematical model claims to demonstrate how seemingly irrational human behavior is determined—and can be predicted by—mathematics. However, it works only as an accomplice (a shill) to the belief that every action is inherently selfish—that no one ever does anything unless they believe it will benefit themselves more than anyone else.

Turns out, Game Theory does accurately describe human behavior. But not in everyone. In fact, only a small subset of people live their lives and make their decisions in accordance with the patterns predicted by Game Theory.

The subset of humans this theory applies to are con-men and the observed behaviors of some mentally ill patients.

> The players of Game Theory control the stock market,
> epitomizing the very definition of con-men.

Ironically, later in life, when John Nash's schizophrenia was under control with medication, he recanted the entire notion of Game Theory as a flawed model.

But game theory does work in explaining the seemingly irrational moves of the stock market.

And who controls the stock market? Stock brokers, traders and economists whose trades are the only things producing the moves.

A bear market (selling frenzy) happens when their confidence is low. A bull market (buying frenzy) occurs when their confidence is high.

The world economy only functions when consumers' confidence remains high. The talking heads on the investment news channels will say this all the time.

Consumer confidence was down in March. That means we shouldn't look for an economic rebound yet.

Retail investors like you and me, typically end up throwing our money into the market when stock prices are right at the top. When confidence is highest.

The con-man has earned our confidence and we give him our watch. We're willing participants in the con. We've become the marks.

A PEOPLE'S HISTORY OF CAPITALISM

Brokers know this. They look for retail investments to spike. When it does, they apply Game Theory to the equation and sell, sell, sell. They walk away with our watch.

Market tops occur just as predicted by economists behaving according to the mathematics of Game Theory.

Retail investors also sell near absolute bottoms, marking the lowest level of confidence. That's when brokers buy, buy, buy.

Con artists.

E*con*omists.

So dark the con of the e*con*omy.

The players of Game Theory control the stock market, epitomizing the very definition of con-men: exploiting characteristics of the human psyche such as greed, both dishonesty and honesty, vanity, compassion, credulity, irresponsibility, naivety.

We the People are the marks, and this is the ultimate con-game.

ECONOMICS
FOR
DUMMIES

BEFORE I had a fundamental understanding of economics, I used to think that even if money didn't exist, things would work on their own.

Unemployed construction workers still possess the skills necessary to build new bridges or repair our infrastructure. Our oil-operated machines still exist. They don't need money to function, only oil.

Money doesn't have skills or possess manpower. It doesn't combust. It doesn't have intelligence. It can't create new technology, or do any of the fundamental things required for building a civilization.

Money doesn't do anything. So why should the absence of money hinder our efforts, stop *progress* in its tracks?

Because our economy is based on neither skills nor labor, production nor products, but on an abstraction: fiat (paper) money.

The problem with paper money is that, almost irrespective of its relationship with Gold, paper currency has no tangible value at all.

Gold really doesn't have much *intrinsic* value either. It's a materialist symbol of status essentially based on nothing except a perception of beauty. Oh, and it's a highly efficient conductor of electricity that remains free of corrosion. (But who cared about that before Steve Jobs started creating jobs?).

◇

MONEY PROVIDES MATERIALISTIC motivation for workers who earn income through labor.

But labor—the most valuable component of an economy—is

merely a slave in an economy based on an abstraction.

In that kind of economy, he who controls the abstraction—fiat (paper) money—is king.

◇

THERE ARE ONLY a few key ways that power can be consolidated in a civilization, placing one definitive ruler (or class) in control.

Among them are:
- Militarily (those who control the biggest, best-trained army.)
- Religiously (the King has a divine right; obey or burn in hell.)
- Agriculturally (those who grow and hoard the food.)
- Intellectually (Rarely. "Smart makes right" just doesn't rhyme.)

And, finally, a Capitalist society is controlled:
- Economically (ruled by the rich).

Farmers are poor, construction workers are unemployed;
Everyone who produces the essentials are peasants.
Inventors of artificial wealth are aristocrats.

That means the majority of wealth today is accumulated by people who sell insurance, give loans or invest in the stock market. In that type of up-side down pyramid society, farmers are poor, construction workers are unemployed, and everyone who produces the things necessary for survival are peasants; while bankers who produce vehicles for artificial wealth-creation become the aristocracy.

In this society, massive accumulations of fiat money are hoarded by people who ... well, make fiat money. Not by people who make wealth.

I would say, to make things equitable, the purchasing power of your money should be determined proportionate to the amount of money you have.

If a can of corn costs $1 for a person who has $100, then a

can of corn (which must still have the same value) should cost $10 to a person who has $1,000.

But that would never work. Oh, well.

◇

PEOPLE WHO HOARD money have been described as, well, hoarders. So why do hoarders hoard? Psychologists tell us it's a symptom of Obsessive Compulsive Disorder. Whether it's money or junk, hoarders hoard because they need to.

So, ok, fine, let the OCD Capitalists keep their hoards of money.

It's not worth anything anyway. We just have to stop believing them when they tell us it is.

But this is not some form of Marxism or Communism where everyone shares everything equally because no one has anything.

The stock market measures how much money the richest among us are hoarding.

Money is not wealth. Wealth can and should be accumulated based on varying values of real labor. Real wealth is produced by labor, making and maintaining the things that are actually needed for people to survive.

Fiat money accumulated in other ways shouldn't share equal value with wealth.

We have made a mockery of money. While money *can* be used to measure wealth, we have corrupted that concept and today mistake money for wealth itself.

Farmers can still produce food and unemployed construction workers still have the skills necessary to maintain bridges, even in a "recession." A recession caused by a severe drought is one thing. A recession caused by a falling stock market is quite another.

The stock market is only a measure of how much money the richest among us are hoarding. What the stock market really seems to measure is the disparity between the amount of money made by the rich and the amount of money earned by the poor. Essentially, the stock market and the value of money share an inverse relationship.

The higher the stock market, the less value our dollars have.

When a stock market collapses, nothing has fundamentally changed in value or in anyone's ability to produce anything, feed everyone or affected our capacity for survival. Farmers still farm. Skills do not diminish.

Before I had a fundamental understanding of economics, I used the think that in the absence of money, things would still work on their own.

Now I realize that *only* in the absence of money are things able to work on their own.

It's a Question of Money

THE stalled economy today is a result of the profit motive not being satisfied.

Infrastructure projects, space programs, educational programs, scientific research, the advancement of civilization are all at a relative stand-still because the people who have all the money to fund these things don't see profit in financing these initiatives.

The money hoarders' only goal is to spend their money in a way to make the biggest financial return as possible. Flying to the moon is not profitable. (Not until we can put a McDonald's there.)

Act now and build America for 0% APR
for the first six months!

Governments are non-profit, so they tax and spend, which is what they should do. Their motivation for spending is purely for the betterment of the society they govern—To give their people the chance at better lives.

But for us, wealth is confused with money. And all money is in the hands of a few private Capitalists. And the only thing that can possibly entice them to spend a dime is the promise of profit, the promise of two dimes in return—a return of more money.

Infrastructure projects, space programs, educational programs, the advancement of civilization—none of them are inherently money makers. They don't provide a financial *return*. That's why they're not good *investments*. That's why they don't get done.

It takes wealth to build and advance civilization and create better lives for everyone. That's never going to happen as long as we confuse money with wealth and let people motivated by profit keep all the money.

◇

WE NEED TO remember that we can *use* money as a tool to create a social structure that benefits everyone.

A truly prosperous, affluent, altruistic, philanthropic society can provide a real safety net and security for everyone—the very thing we think only money can provide. If these things were assured, guaranteed, no one would need money to achieve them.

> Let's transfer money into programs so there's
> less money for rich people to hoard.
> Let's use it so they can't invest it.

We need to stop thinking in terms of *spending* money. We need to start thinking in terms of *using* money as a tool to transform society, which creates infinitely more wealth than using money to make money. Yet we are obsessed with the idea that a monetary return is the only acceptable return on an investment.

The Capitalists are transforming wealth into money.

We can decide to take it back and transform wealth into progress.

Yes, we would *lose* money doing it. But that's the point: to transfer wealth not into the hands of the richest, but to transfer it into programs like eduction, science, art, and civilization. Let's transfer wealth into these programs so there's less money for rich people to hoard.

Let's spend it so they can't invest it.

As it is, they are transforming all the labor of humanity, all the work all of us does everyday, into dollars. And that makes no sense.

That work should not be valued in dollars.

If we insist on using money, people should be paid all of what their activities are worth. Today's standard corporate model is for an employee to get a salary equivalent to 25% of the money he makes for the company.

With that model, 500 of the richest humans collect all the money. Such a small group should not have the power to decide how all the wealth created by all of us is used.

We should step back from that system and simply say, "This isn't right."

And stop it.

◇

WE MIGHT DO so by learning to stop thinking that civilization building can only by financed with money.

Civilization building doesn't need to be *financed* in the first place. Act now and build America for 0% APR for the first six months!

The Capitalists are transforming wealth into money.
Let's take it back and transform wealth into progress.

All that's required to build civilization up is a willing group of people who can be fed, sheltered and have all their needs met in return for their daily activities. No, not *barely* met as in the case of slavery, which gives the slaves just enough to keep them alive.

Everyone should be well-provided for, not by money, but by the things we really need for shelter, security and happiness. It can all be done without the use of money.

We can't eat money; we can't drink money; we can't build shelters out of dollar bills. We don't need money. We need food, water, shelter, other people, sunlight and nature to live happily ever after.

A PEOPLE'S HISTORY OF CAPITALISM

It's only a dream. I know. And it will never happen, at least not until the far, far distant future.

But it's important to understand, to conceptualize, that it *is* possible to build a society not based on money. It *is* possible to build a society based on the desire for a better life for all.

Economics in Wonderland

IMAGINE two mirrors facing each other. Now imagine walking between them and staring at infinite reflections of yourself. What would happen if you took a $100 bill out of your pocket? Would you instantly become a millionaire? According to Wall Street bankers, the answer is yes. They even have a fancy word for the infinite reflections of a dollar: derivatives.

It's absurd. You know and I know you still only have $100. Yet the 1% of people who live in this Economic Wonderland have sold the rest of us a bill of goods.

And we've bought it.

The Two Mirrors Theory of Economics

THIS is the lie our entire economy is based on:

Since the 1850s, we've believed the idea that civilization itself is based solely on economics. Believing that, we've been busy bees building an entire civilization that *is* based on economics.

And we've succeeded. Our myopic civilization looks at the world through a fun house mirror that distorts the image and reflects it back on itself, reinforcing the delusion.

But with our rapidly destabilizing economy, it's only a matter of time before the mirrors crack and bring all of civilization crashing down all around us.

Economic Alchemy

WHAT, exactly, does it mean that our Global Gross Domestic Product is $60 trillion dollars?

It means, basically, that by the way economists figure it, all of the things humans do in any given year—all our labor, all the food we grow, all the buildings we construct, all the clothes we sew, all the cars we build, all the products we produce, all the crap we buy and the junk that breaks and gets fixed—all of it, together, is worth $60 trillion.

For simplicity's sake, let's just say there's a combined workforce of 7 billion people. (Which there isn't because 7 billion is how many of us there are on Earth in 2011, and so in terms of labor, that's not subtracting the elderly, infirm, unemployed and figuring out where child labor laws are disobeyed.)

But just for argument sake, let's say a workforce of 7 billion produces $60 trillion worth of labor each year. That would mean every man, woman and child should be earning $8,000/year.

Global GDP is a measly $60 trillion;
the global derivatives market is $1.2 quadrillion!

In reality, the bottom 85% of humanity (in economic terms) earns less than $2,000/year.

The top 10% of humanity earns over $25,000/year. And if you earn $50,000/year or more, you are in the economic top 1% of all the people on Earth.

And then there are those 1% of all Americans earn over $100,000/year. Those folks are living in the economic top .003% of all 7 billion of us.

And then there are, of course, the 500 or so individual, transnational multi-billionaires.

If the global GDP is only $60 trillion per year, how can there be *any* multi-billionaires at all?

Ah, well, you see, their money doesn't factor into the global GDP number. GDP accounts for labor and products which are actually *produced*. Most billionaires' money comes, largely, not from production, but from money itself—winning bets in the stock market, capital gains, interest, dividends and so on.

While global GDP is a measly $60 trillion, the global derivatives market is said to be $1.2 quadrillion! (One quadrillion is 1,000 trillion).

So that means something like the top 1/75,000 of the top 1% of the world's economic elite are placing bets in excess of 1,000 times more than the entire amount of money currently in circulation. And that's every year.

Most billionaires' money comes, largely, not from production, but from money itself—winning bets in the stock market.

And what are they betting their money on?

They're betting their money on, well, money.

The best way to explain a *Derivatives Market for Dummies* is essentially to say that gambling in derivatives is like holding $100 in your hand and betting against its value. Your bet is that the $100 you hold in your hand will only be worth $99 at some point in the future.

And since you are betting 1,000 times the amount of money in circulation, for every variation of a single penny in the price of a single dollar, you've just "made" $10.

And for every $10 fabricated in this way, the value of every $1 of existing money in circulation goes down by another, say 1/10 of a penny. And so you make $1 more based on nothing other than the fact that you just made $10 a half second ago.

But these billionaires aren't using dollar bills to place their bets. They're not even betting with $100 bills.

The bets they're placing carry unfathomable stakes. They're

betting tens of thousands and hundreds of millions of dollars on a single crapshoot.

So for every variation of 1/10th of a penny in the value of a single $1, their bets pay off millions, if not tens of millions of dollars.

Just, poof, materializing right there out of thin air, every second of every day.

◇

EVERY DOLLAR YOU'VE ever paid in interest is a derivative in its simplest form. Interest is money derived from lending money. It's not earned for rendering a service, or even *made*.

It's simply fabricated, made-up. And every dollar that's fabricated, a figment created by interest or gambling, devalues every other existing dollar. Money might not grow on trees, but it can be made right out of thin air.

That's what I'd call economic alchemy.

In fact, *making* money in the derivatives market is exactly the opposite of what it purports to be. For every dollar that's made out of thin air, dollars that are earned become worth proportionately less.

Things carry a value directly related to how hard they are to come by.

But not in today's world.

We have an economy based on financial services. Where the economic elite get richer by the second because they are the economic elite.

RUMPELSTILTSKIN

THERE is a socio-economic movement that has been trending now for about 6,500 years, ever since the dawn of Western Civilization.

This is not the shadow agenda of a "secret society." There's nothing covert about it. The only place it's hiding is right out in the open.

This agenda transcends political parties, religious beliefs, and racial divides. The best ways to describe this movement today is to say its leaders are "Corporatists."

Its leaders have hidden behind various guises in the past and gone by many other names, including "Royalists," "Fascists," "Sovereigns" and even "Monsignor."

They see civilization as no more than a game, and they believe it's monopolized by no more than a handful of key players at any given time.

These players are rarely heads of state. They're rarely interested in power, although it's probably happened.

In general, though, politicians, Monarchs, even Dictators tremble at their feet. In this game, governments are merely figureheads. Heads of state are usually made the fall guy when things go awry.

These players have been cunning over the centuries; they are the Rumpelstiltskin of Civilization, the tricksters.

These players have been cunning throughout the centuries; they are the Rumpelstiltskin of civilization, the tricksters. They have groomed everything from dictatorships to democracies and even the common man to believe they are looking out for us.

They act as though they believe that it is their divine right to be the leaders of human civilization (and I have no doubt some really do believe that).

These players hold the reigns, pull the purse strings of power. They cheat the system. By their influence, power does not rest with the people, or in the hands of the leaders that the people elect. They purchase officials, sometimes buy elections outright.

Rumpelstiltskin has no time to deal with messy, sloppy, democratic elections, whose outcomes aren't assured. Why run for office when you can simply overrun the office?

Even Sovereign monarchs (a term which means, "the king who is above the law") have been bewitched by Rumpel.

◇

RUMPELSTILTSKIN'S LATEST INVENTION is the Free Market. Rumpelstiltskin controls the Free Market, where he spins straw into gold, and makes money grow on trees.

Why buy the milk at retail prices, when you can by the cow wholesale? In fact, why buy the cow wholesale, when you control the market that sets the price of beef?

This is not a conspiracy theory. No one is scheming in dark rooms behind closed doors. There are no Capitalist cronies secret agent shills operating in the dark. No, they operate out in the open.

Their trick is not to lie in hiding, but to deceive the rest of us into believing they are working in everyone's best interest.

Rumpelstiltskin controls the Free Market, where he spins straw into gold, and makes money grow on trees.

All the while, 99% of the world's wealth is hoarded by this 1% of the population. And 99% of the world's population is left squabbling for the scraps from Rumpelstiltskin's table.

There's nothing conspiratorial in that. Ten minutes in the

A PEOPLE'S HISTORY OF CAPITALISM

local library will tell you who the Forbes 500 are. Not all of the Fortune 500 go by the name of Rumple, of course. No, it's just a few bad apples.

They have the wealth to buy the world. And frequently do.

Sometimes they even masquerade as pure Capitalists so we think all they want is money. But it's not.

What they want is all the power that all the money can buy. And all the money all the power can hoard.

In short, they want it all.

They want the monopoly on greed.

They want to be corrupted absolutely.

◇

RUMPELSTILTSKIN HAS RISEN to power and then fallen out of favor only to rise once more.

The pendulum of history always over swings.

Rumpelstiltskin's game of chess has come down to
its final moves. The King of May is in check.

Revolt against Rumpel's control has sparked the modern world's deadliest wars: The American Civil War, the American and French Revolutions, World War I and World War II.

Conflicts are born when inequality in society reaches a fever pitch, when teeter-totter economies pivot on the verge of collapse, and the top 1% equally distributes all the wealth among themselves. Then the elitists themselves start bickering, fancying themselves Gods on Mount Olympus.

Over the past 30 years, Rumpelstiltskin has consolidated power in unprecedented ways, his rise to ascendency endorsed by Imperial Capitalist Globalization.

Today's deadliest game pits Capitalists (Rumpelstiltskin) against democratic governments (the people's last line of defense). Of course this is nothing new. Corporations and Government have been vying for power since the age of the East India Company.

Different strategies have been used by Rumple at different times. In the early 1900s, the strategy involved fascism, the blending of state and corporate interstates. But all that accomplished was World War I.

Rumpelstiltskin has since decided to forego combining forces with government. His new plan is to take government out of the picture all together.

His strategy?

It's what we're seeing today in the financial collapse of Europe and America. It started in a few key second-world countries in South America that no one paid much attention to. That was a trial run. Rumple had his eye on a much bigger prize.

The battle moved into the First World, where Iceland was the first domino to fall when its economy collapsed in early 2008.

Today, Rumpelstiltskin's game of chess has come down to a few final moves. The King of May is in check. (The King of May is the male representation of spring, re-birth, hope and spirit in the Celtic ceremony of Beltane).

Evidence of Rumpelstiltskin's ascendency is most conspicuous in the disparity between rich and poor, which, today is less of a gap and more of a Grand Canyon.

We pawns have revolted many times in the past. But recently, it seems, with our minds addled by television, our credit cards enslaving us to debt, and our obsession with the material world dictating our actions, we can only hope the motivation to change the world isn't as atrophied as we seem to be.

The Second Bailout

WHERE were you when the United States Congress voted on what would come to be called the first bailout, in 2008?

(We must have forgotten this already happened in 1773.)

I was watching CNBC. Yes, the Stock Market Channel.

I didn't know what I was doing. I only knew what was being reported by the talking heads on the talking box—and that I should be afraid—be very afraid—of a global financial meltdown if Congress didn't vote for the bailout.

Well, we all should be afraid of a global financial meltdown, and giving corporations what they want is the very thing that's going to cause it.

You need a much deeper awareness of economics and politics than the average person has in order to notice the man behind the curtain. I should know; I was watching CNBC when he reared his head. And I didn't see a thing.

The media was telling us, "Pay no attention to the banks behind the bailout!"

When's the last time you got all the dominos to collapse without first spending an hour meticulously lining them up?

And so, many of us obediently didn't. At first.

At first many of us believed what we were told: it's all the fault of those lazy delinquents not paying their mortgage!

But while we thought this situation was unique to America, if we'd been paying any attention at all, we'd have known this was happening already, everywhere else.

Ours was one of the last shoes to drop.

From South America to Iceland to Greece and Italy to England and finally landing in America, there was a Corporate war against the State being waged, and the People were caught in the middle.

What happened on each of these front lines was a well-coordinated financial collapse and then made to look like the fault of governments.

When's the last time you got all the dominos to collapse without first spending an hour meticulously lining them up?

And even then they don't always fall the way you planned.

They have to be lined up just so.

Oh, yes, this was a well-planned, coordinated assault. Things fit together too perfectly to have not been planned.

OK, that might be a bit of a conspiracy theory.

I'm not on a political rant. I'm on an economic rant,
which is far less politically correct.

But the truth is Financial Executives and CEOs are bankrupting the economies of the world by making everyone slaves to debt. Governments, people, other corporations, sometimes even their own corporations.

CEOs are quietly pocketing all the money and watching every other institution go down in flames.

And a lot of all that money just disappears into the black hole of deep pockets just as quickly and quietly as it appeared out of thin air in the first place.

Then another bubble bursts, the financial corporations cry bankruptcy, and go groveling at the feet of world governments.

◇

THERE'S A CAPITALIST koan that goes like this: A CEO and a congressman are having dinner with Joe Blow. As the congressman is listening to Joe explain his troubles, the Capitalist is quietly eating everything in the breadbasket on the table.

When there's only one roll left, the Capitalist turns to Joe and says, "Watch out for this sleazy politician! He's gunna eat your last piece of bread!"

◇

IN THE UNITED States, there were actually two votes in Congress before the first corporate bailout package was passed on October 3, 2008.

The first vote shot the bailout down.

That vote reflected the deluge of calls that flooded the White House switchboard, almost unanimously against the bailout.

At least some people were paying attention and had enough sense to make their voices heard.

> The best way to spot a lie is to notice contradictions, inconsistencies in the story.

Needless to say, the Corporations didn't like Congress' first answer. So they bribed some Senators and did some other shenanigans.

A second vote was scrambled together in just a couple days. It went the other way this time and the Corporations got their way, People be damned.

It was nothing short of an economic *coup d'état* of the United States.

Depending on where we go from here, historians may look back on that day and equate it to the assassination of Julius Caesar. That's the day the Republic of Rome fell and the Roman Empire began.

The TARP vote on October 3rd, 2008 may be viewed by future historians as the day the United States of America became the United Corporations of America.

I won't dwell on this point further. There are plenty of books and documentaries that will fill in the details where I've painted only broad strokes. Start with Michael Moore's *Capitalism: A Love Story*.

I'm not on a political rant. I'm on an economic rant, which is far less politically correct.

◇

LEARNING THE TRUTH of all this in the following years was like stepping into a parallel universe. The world I'd been living in, the one the media had painted for me, was a complete and utter fabrication.

If all the people and all the governments are going bankrupt, where did the money go?

I'd known something was rotten in the state of Denmark, but I didn't know what. But something. And the media wasn't helping me figure out what.

So, what woke me up? The best way to spot a lie is to notice contradictions, inconsistencies in the story. So I asked myself, "Ok, if all the people and all the governments are going bankrupt, where did all the money go?" It seemed it couldn't have just vanished. It must have gone somewhere.

The answer jolted me awake. Some had evaporated into thin air from whence it came. That proved there was a pyramid scheme in affect, which The Powers that Be claimed there wasn't. But most of it ended up in the already-deep pockets of the millionaires and billionaires—proving they were behind the scheme, which The Powers that Be claimed they weren't.

Another contradiction was revealed on a silver platter while watching "the news" (Yes, still CNBC, but by 2010 I was spying behind enemy lines, not drinking the Kool-Aid.)

The anchor affectionately known as the Money Honey claimed that, paraphrasing, "The best financial analysts in the world don't know why this financial meltdown occurred. Economists don't believe in the myth of a bubble, and think, from the best they can ascertain, that economies just have to correct like this every once in a while. It last happened in the 1930s with the Great Depression. I guess it just happens every 80 years or so. That's just the Free

Market doing its job."*

No really, she said that.

Huh!? She expected me to believe that the best financial economists in the world—who invented derivatives and annuities and toxic mortgages, oh my!—didn't know why this all happened!? These are smart people. Too smart for our own good.

I didn't buy that they didn't know.

I was fully awake now, all the apathy jolted out of me.

And I stepped out of that parallel reality maintained by the Corporate-controlled media.

At first I didn't believe it. Then I was angry. Now I hope that at least one good thing can come out of all this.

If it woke me up, I hope it woke up some other people, too.

I hope.

---

* As of 2011, the Money Honey is still asleep. In October 2011, she asked, paraphrasing, "These Occupy Wall Street Guys ... What the heck are we protesting?"

Ah, absolute money ... corrupts absolutely ... and causes absolute ignorance.

"The pendulum always over swings."

— *Experience*

"We like strong, happy people
Who don't think there's something wrong with pride.
Work makes them free, and we spread that freedom far and wide,
And the Empire grows."

— *Dar Williams*
Empire

PART 3

The Mind of Greed

Survival of the Fittest Capitalists

SURVIVAL of the fittest is a Capitalist ideology. It was set forth by Darwin around the very same time as Marshall's *Principles of Economics*. It grew out of the same world view that gave rise to Imperialist Capitalism.

Evolution takes as one of its key premises that all of life is in competition with all other life on the planet and, more importantly, with the other members of its own species.

Yet today, we see greater evidence that life is actually based on cooperation, not competition. But this matters little. At the dawn of evolution, that's not how the best minds of the day saw things. And once a paradigm is established, it becomes much harder to overturn than it was to create.

Imperialist Capitalist is the ultimate
mechanism for survival of *only* the fittest.
Competition only reigns supreme in a Capitalist Society.

Western thinking at the time included three main premises: Capitalism is King, Church and State need to be separated, and through our best machines created during the Scientific and Industrial Revolution, we could tame, control and understand nature.

Western minds, fresh out of 1,000 year of bondage by the Church and Feudalism, were intent on finding an alternate hypothesis for how the world worked that did not involve the existence of God— or indeed, anything spiritual beyond the comprehension of Science. At the same time, the combination of Church and State was being replaced with something even more dangerous: the combination of Capitalism and State (later coming to be known as fascism).

From the absolute rejection of spirituality and the acceptance of material wealth, Capitalism created a *dog-eat-dog* world which worked beautifully for the Capitalists, satisfying their primary motivation: greed. Since that way was working so well for them—better than anything we'd tried before—it must be the only way to live. It must apply universally and reveal a fundamental law of nature.

Out of the convergence of all these ideas, we developed an Imperialist view of Evolution.

Imperialist Capitalism is the ultimate incarnation of survival of the fittest. Competition only reigns supreme in a Capitalist Society.

Arguably, survival of the fittest applies exclusively to Capitalism.

Adopting an Imperialist view of evolution gave us fresh incentives and greater leave to amorally devour all the people who stood in the way of the holy march of Capitalism. It was a *dog-eat-dog* world, after all. And Capitalism has been evolving ever since into an ever-more ruthless beast.

When the Tide Comes In....

THE Biblical Great Flood occurred 8,000-10,000 years ago, and today the waters are about the crest.

I'm referring to the Great Flood metaphorically.

The Flood has both historical and mythological significance as an analogy for the tide of human events. The resurgence of civilization after the historical Great Flood marked the beginning of The Great Flood of Western Thought.

It's been during the 6,500 of Empire building since that the world has experienced the meteoric rise of Western Culture.

And it's just possible that in our lifetime—yours and mine—we will finally see the waters of that Great Flood of Western Thought flood the world again.

The last Aborigines are all but extinct. The last remnants of an ancient way of life have been swept away.

And sea level literally is rising as a symptom of Global Warming. We are seeing the climax of our modern way of life, finding ourselves on the backside of a classic, parabolic trajectory towards collapse.

◇

WHEN WE COLLAPSE and we will, whether it be a fractal collapse caused by Global Warming, or the end of oil; or by a gradual shift in worldview that saves us in the 11th hour from the fate we are careening towards—When we collapse, what will the next incarnation of civilization say about us? 10,000 years in the future, will we even be remembered? Will anyone be around who remembers how we carved The Four Heads of Mount Rushmore? Or will they scratch their own heads and wonder how the heck we carved faces in a solid stone mountainside without machines, tools, writing, electricity, or even the wheel (as we say about the Egyptian Sphinx)?

Will future historians misplace 200-300 years of history and believe Native American rock art was created by the same people who constructed Mount Rushmore? Both exist in the same region, and it's very easy to misplace 300 years here and there if you're an archeologist digging back through 10,000 years of fossil evidence. Incidentally, there is no known way to Carbon-14 date rock.

Will future civilizations know the Roman Colosseum was built 1,000 years before the great Cathedrals of Europe? Or will 1,000 years be lost in the great melting pot of the geological record?

And most importantly of all, will anyone learn from our mistakes?

◇

THE HISTORICAL GREAT Flood was likely triggered by a worldwide cataclysmic event. Perhaps a meteor. Fringe science even suggests an ancient nuclear war.

Whatever it was, I have no doubt there were entire civilizations wiped out by the global calamity—civilizations we have absolutely no record of today.

They existed so long ago, and on the other side of such a cataclysm, that knowledge of them is completely and forever shrouded by the mists of time.

So how can we learn from their mistakes when we don't even know what mistakes they made or that they even existed at all?

FINAL APPROACH!

DURING the first 3.5 billion years of the Earth's existence, there was no life whatsoever. Molten lava from the planet's core spewed through volcanic fissures to the surface, making this Hadean Earth an inferno inhospitable to life (even to extremophiles who would appear later).

When the Earth's fires tamed, a new onslaught began. During the next half billion years or so, the fire of life was kindled.

For millions of years after that, species slithered and squirmed, flew, swam, galloped, scampered, writhed, wiggled and crawled. But no species, from any walk of life, used, invented, or conceived at all of anything remotely like that which we call *technology* today.

Then the real storm erupted.

Over the next 300,000 years, one species evolved who discovered the secret of harnessing fire for itself, that age-old Hadeanistic ravisher of the Earth.

Humanity's love of fire became the root of all technology.

The degree of heat our fires burned at would dictate which metals we could forge into which alloys and how much strength could be infused into those metallic hybrids. And, whosoever wielded weapons made from the strongest alloys would come to conquer the world.

Stones and slings had given way to Bronze swords in perhaps 100,000 years.

Bronze gave way to Iron in perhaps 10,000 years.

Iron gave way to Steel in just 3,000 years.

The rise of technology was meteoric. The uncountable millennia separating successive quantum leaps of civilization building diminished asymptotically. The intervening millennia could now be counted. (Asymptotically is the inverse of exponentially—approaching zero instead of infinity.)

Then the time-span shrunk to less than a single human life.

When we ran out of new metals to forge, still we figured out how to make fire burn hotter. Now we were creating nuclear reactions.

Many of us thought we'd surely destroy ourselves with that incarnation of fire.

But I don't think it will be a weapon at all which will destroy us. I believe it will be our mindset, ourselves.

Today the time span of change has diminished to within the blink of a human eye.

I'm not sure I want to know what comes next.

A PEOPLE'S HISTORY OF CAPITALISM

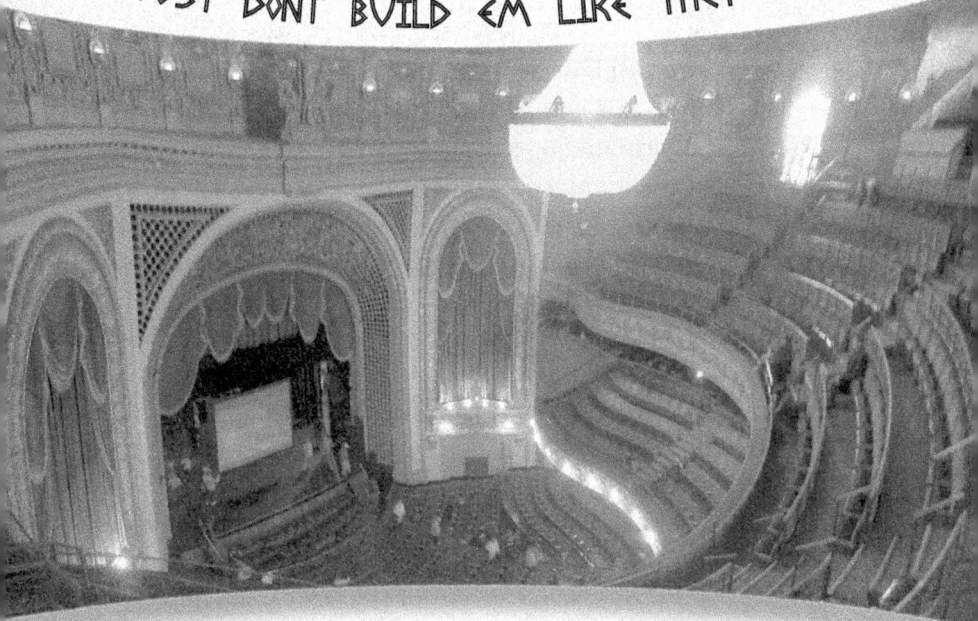

THEY JUST DONT BUILD EM LIKE THEY USED TO

ONUMENTAL stone amphitheaters and Imperial palaces were being built as far back as 5,000 years ago, perhaps even earlier. Rome had its Colosseum, the Parthenon and an elaborate system of aqueducts.

Mayans and Egyptians built Pyramids.

Further back still, ruins of ancient civilizations at Mohenjo Daro and Babylon hold a myriad of megalithic temples.

Colossal stone and marble façades adorn the breathtaking architecture of Greece.

Today, modern engineering is as inspired as it was in the ancient world ..... but our building practices are comparatively pathetic.

Our bridges are in constant need of repair, always threatening us with collapse. Keep in mind the Spynx, Pyramids, Roman Colloseum and ancient Greek temples have survived for millennia. No one so much as applied a new layer of caulk for 5,000 years, and they're doing just fine.

But today we take shortcuts.

BEFORE OUR LOVE affair with cutting corners took off, the zenith of construction projects in our own civilization climaxed in the late 19th to early 20th centuries.

That was Empire building at its finest. (Not that Empire building is a particularly noble enterprise, but it does accomplish impressive feats and makes notable marks on the historical record. It's never that great for the plebeians who provide the slave labor during the construction process of course.)

Captains of Industry were trying to outshine each other by building taller and taller stone structures in the early 1900s.

John D. Rockerfeller enthusiastically poured his ill-gotten industrial wealth into construction of the Rockerfeller plaza in the 1930s.

The photo on the preceding page depicts the historic Pabst Theater in Milwaukee, built in 1895, and widely regarded as the most "glorious" theater in America. One can't help but marvel at the impressive architecture, a shrine for the arts. Truly impressive that a society was so prosperous it could pour so many resources into a theater.

And it did require a lot of resources. We started to realize that despite the promise of immortality that great construction projects held for their architects, these really big things were eating into profits big time.

There was a little bit of downtime in our obsession with monument building. Then an idea that probably would occur only to a Capitalist was born—shortcuts.

Steel came along at the same time, which was far cheaper than concrete. Greed and steel created a strong alliance which led to the unbridled rise of Skyscrapers. This Empire in the Sky arose in the 1970s, financed by short cuts, steel and Capitalism.

According to Matthias Altwicker, a German-American professor of architecture at the New York Institute of Technology, much clearer lines between safety and economics exist in most other countries.

For instance, the World Trade Center couldn't have been built in Germany where safety codes are much stricter. Concrete is used a lot more than steel, despite the added cost.

Steel Skyscrapers are no doubt impressive, despite their propensity to collapse when the engineers tell us they won't.

Gigantic iron ocean liners are also quite a sight to behold, despite their propensity to sink when engineers tell us they can't. (The Titanic used inferior rivets to save money, directly leading to its sinking.)

Space shuttles are a testament to our reach for the stars, despite their propensity to explode on take-off ... and re-entry—even though Scientists never see it coming.

Out of all the designs for the Space Shuttle (there were at least 80), the least expensive was used.

Even things that aren't worth doing are worth doing well.

But here's the rub: It's not the engineers or the scientists who are to blame. It's the companies who commission them to find the cheapest way instead of the best way. There's enough blame to spread around to the contractors who build the things, just trying to survive in our profit-oriented society's cutthroat fever fueled by Capitalism.

To underbid their competitors, contractors cut corners. He who finds the shortest shortcut wins the race.

◇

FAST FORWARD 100 years from the construction of the historic, stone Pabste Theatre and look to its modern day doppelgängers. Theaters today (largely for mass-distribution *movies*, not experiencing one-of-a kind live entertainment) look like giant cubes, without pomp, circumstance, or finesse.

Once-glorious cathedrals were thought to be a testament to God's Kingdom on Earth. Today, they too are shaped like boxes.

Once-luxurious Victorian mansions were really something to see in their day. They set themselves apart by feeding into the vanity of their owners with their unique, often eccentric designs (think Frank Lloyd Wright.) These have all been replaced by dry-walled suburbia, manufactured houses and condo associations where every building looks identical. Did communism prevail after all?

The nation-building and Empire expansion that we saw into the beginning of the 20th century is part of a by-gone era. It has deteriorated into nation-maintaining.

Maintaining an empire is not nearly as glorious (or profitable) as building it up in the first place.

Empire building used to be the holy work of Imperialists seeking immortality. Now the holy work is making money.

Now, I'm no fan of Empire building myself. But it seems that even things that aren't worth doing are worth doing well.

If you must to do it, at least do it right.

Yet today it's merely a question of maintaining an infrastructure that will collapse as quickly as it was erected if not maintained on an on-going, continual, resource-sapping daily basis. Which ends up being more expensive that doing it right in the first place.

You can spot a myopic (near-sighted) Capitalist a mile away.

The trick is doing everything as cheaply as possible.

That's why they just don't build things like they used to.

MY IMMORTAL MONEY

WE used to build great things because Egyptian Pharaohs, Popes, Warlords and Captains of Industry wanted to immortalize themselves for all time. Then we realized we didn't need to build things or make things to gain immortality. We didn't even need to build things or make things to make money. We just needed to create "endowment funds" and "trust funds." These, theoretically, are the funds which keep on giving, ensuring the immortal prosperity of a few select bloodlines, Capitalism without End, A-men.

Buildings will crumble, but money will last forever.

We sought a great City of Gold when we invaded the "new world." We knew it must exist! It didn't. But no matter! We'll just build our own. And so we did with the invention of the stock market. Only it's a city built out of fool's gold.*

We were not only on a heroic *quest* for immortality, we believed it was our Divine Right. And since we thought we were so entitled, some of us decided we shouldn't have to work for it.

Why toil at building things? We're too omnipotent for that! Buildings will crumble, but money will last forever.

And that is the pinnacle of foolishness and a recipe for self-destruction. Ironically, the very monetary scheme we've built to immortalize ourselves (The Great Pyramid of Paper) will crumble long before the Great Pyramid at Giza.

---

* Fools gold is actually a mineral called pyrite. Which, appropriately, sounds like 'Pirate,' though there is actually no entomological link.

THE SYSYPHUS SYNDROME

WHEN the first Captains of Industry set about the Mass Industrialization of the world, did they consider—in fact could they even fathom—how much upkeep and maintenance and repairs would forever be required?

If there's one thing Capitalists are good at, it's mass producing profit. If there's one thing Capitalists are really bad at, it's thinking ahead—at least beyond the next quarterly earnings statement.

And yet the true legacy of their industrialization scheme is repair and upkeep and maintenance, oh my!

Increasingly elaborate networks of infrastructure are perpetually expanded to allow for the mass transit of mass produced merchandise.

Water purification plants, waste management facilities, bridges, and roads are all luxuries that have become necessities in this fragile civilization we've built for ourselves.

They have become the artificial life support system in a world of ever-increasing population. Without these technological inventions and infrastructure, populations around the world never would have exploded to the levels they're at today. And without the constant, daily upkeep and maintenance of our life support system, the world would see a 90% population drop almost overnight. It would make the Black Death look like the common cold.

Long after we've abandoned our civilization,
or it collapses under its own weight, someone's
still going to have to maintain it all.

Capitalists keep dreaming up new ways of profiting off the necessary repairs.

While the automotive industry profits from the sale of new cars, oil companies capitalize on the price of gas, and mechanics make money repairing cars .... just where in the world would all those cars go to if not for the roads?

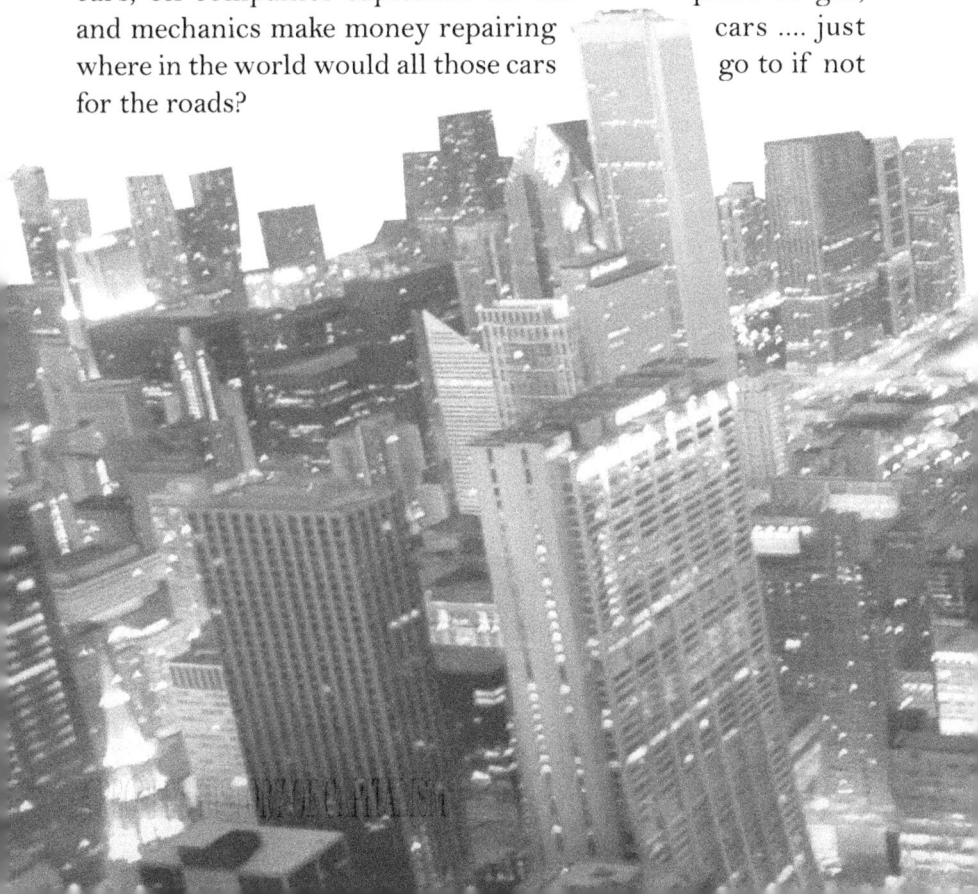

If it weren't for the government- sponsored road construction projects, the continual need for repairs would sap all the profit out of selling cars and drilling for oil.

People don't take their cars to work, they take the highways and byways. And who creates, repairs and resurfaces those arteries?

It's a dirty job, but somebody's got to do it. Yes, but who's going to *pay* for it?

The government! quoth the Capitalists.

And who's going to make money on it?

We are! quoth the Capitalists.

So the government contracts out road work and bridge repair and a lot of other work to the private sector. And where does the money come from to pay those private contractors? Tax dollars.

And the CEOs of contracting companies keep the lion's share of the revenue. In Capitalism, the flow of money goes in one direction only.

Government subsidies of (mostly) the wrong kind of companies ensures that river keeps on rolling along.

So while the companies sell you the car to drive, the government steps in where Capitalists fear to tread.

It is a prime example of privatizing the profit and socializing the debt.

In Capitalism, the flow of money goes
in one direction only.

Did Capitalists think this through when they first industrialized the world? Or did they perfect this game of cat-and-mouse along the way?

It's the same story with our water supply and so many other aspects of the Commons. If water doesn't undergo a rigorous purification process (performed by the government-run public works department), then all the pollution of industrial waste renders all our water non-potable.

NOW CONSIDER THE bigger picture. Forget about who performs the maintenance, who pays, and who profits.

What if *nobody* did?

If the governments of the world were to stop footing the bill for constantly cleaning up after industry, there would be none of us left to buy anything.

Without waste management and water filtration, urban areas become overrun with refuse and waste. Nuclear power plants quickly go into meltdown without daily supervision.

Long after we've abandoned our civilization, or it collapses under its own weight, maintenance will still be necessary!

Nuclear waste, for instance, buried deep in the Earth, will remain toxic for tens of thousands of years.

Today we're beginning to trap Carbon Dioxide deep inside stratified limestone to prevent it from getting released into the atmosphere where it would quickly exacerbate global warming.

But even if it's 20,000 years from now, that CO_2 is going to get into the atmosphere eventually.

Capitalists are just betting they won't be around to worry about it.

Do we need to put up big yellow signs imprinted with the universal symbol for toxic waste in order to serve as a warning to future civilizations? Forbidden Zone Ahead!

Not Zone. Zones. They pockmark the Earth.

If the governments of the world were to stop footing the bill for constantly cleaning up after industry, there would be none of us left to buy anything.

Indeed, maintaining the infrastructure of an industrialized society is much more than a full time job.

In former Western colonies like Madagascar (abandoned by French colonials in the 1950s), people today are living in squalor, poverty and unsanitary urban areas far worse than anything they'd known before the unmistakable footprint of Imperialist Capitalism was set in stone.

The entirety of the so-called "Third World" is the inescapable result of the end of urban upkeep and industrial maintenance. Abject poverty spreads across the land.

The same thing happens in "ghost-towns" in America, and I don't mean just the ones in Western films with tumbleweeds blowing through the streets.

There are modern cities and towns that lie abandoned all over the country. Most are abandoned when coal mines fail.

A few short years after the auto industry shut down plants en masse in 2009, effected towns and cities resemble Third World countries.

> The entirety of the so-called "Third World" is the inescapable result of the end of urban upkeep and industrial maintenance.

Poverty and hopelessness are born in these decimated areas.

None of this natural. It's the inescapable aftermath of a once-industrialized civilization that became utterly dependent on an infrastructure that became so expansive that it collapsed under its own weight.

Industrialized societies lock themselves into perpetual boom-and-bust cycles.

And it doesn't take much to go bust.

The infrastructure we give our lives to requires daily maintenance. It's always an uphill climb.

Meanwhile, we tell ourselves, don't worry, it'll all be worth it! You'll see! Utopia is just around the corner!

◇

WE STARTED CLIMBING this steep slope because some of

us weren't content living as hunter-gatherers. That's when we started farming.

But that was hard work, too.

Thus began our endless quest to invent new and better technologies to make our lives better. Many of those technologies are created to solve problems created by earlier technologies.

And they layer upon each other. Layer after layer after layer. And we become dependent on them as our pyramid of technological infrastructure becomes more and more complex. The uphill climb gets steeper and steeper.

In the Greek Myth of *Sisyphus*, King Sisyphus is punished to roll a boulder up a steep hill for all eternity. Each time, just before he reaches to the top, the incline becomes so steep that the bolder starts rolling backward under the gravity of its own weight.

So Sisyphus must start all again.

A GREAT PYRAMID OF PAPER

LOOKING back on it all, future historians see that the great mountain of Capitalist civilization was shaped like a pyramid and made out of dollar bills, and it was levitating high above the ground.

Capitalists beheld a great sight from their vantage point. Their civilization was floating, no longer tethered to the Earth at all.

The mountain of civilization was shaped like a pyramid and made out of dollar bills, and it was levitating high above the ground.

Gangly roots protruded from the underside of the mountain, dangling freely in the air, no longer able to reach the Earth below, which is where they had always gotten their nutrients from.

The profits of Capitalism build

a

great

top-heavy

pyramid of paper

higher and higher and higher.

Meanwhile, most people were standing atop a series of unstable platforms built on the sloped sides of the pyramid. There were two kinds of platforms supporting the 7 billion of us: towering skyscrapers swaying in the wind, and domed-shaped Government Capitol buildings. Trying to stand on either platform was challenging. It was very hard to keep your balance. Some of us were running along narrow suspension bridges spanning huge gulches between the roofs of all those buildings we had erected.

One day someone decided to look up. And he saw that the hovering pyramid of civilization wasn't floating in mid-air at all. He saw taut electrical cables acting like guy-wires anchoring the pyramid to a fleet of airplanes flying overhead, which were being perpetually re-fueled in mid air. (They were using fuel faster than they could be re-fueled).

Back on the sloped sides of the pyramid, pumpjacks stood astride oil wells that burrowed so deeply into the pyramid that the shafts extended right through to the bottom of the floating mountain.

Capitalists loomed over those fissures and peered down through them. They saw that the Earth that we'd forgotten far, far below looked pretty small from way up here. They instantly knew just how long the fall back to the ground would be.

"Hey, we better make sure we keep this thing afloat! *I think* we can do it! *I think* we can make sure those pumpjacks keep working to produce enough oil to keep those planes fueled and flying. *I think* we can make sure those guy-wires don't snap! Even if we can't do all that forever, *I know* we can make a profit trying! We'll set the price to keep this thing afloat really high. Because people will know that they'll be an even greater price to pay if we don't."

And we're paying the price alright.

Meanwhile, the profit the Capitalists make by keeping us afloat build our great pyramid of paper ever taller. And, like a helium balloon, all that paper money keeps inflating, taking us ever higher. Up, up and away we go.

How Oil Ended Slavery

THE rise of all great civilizations has been fueled by slave labor. Slavery was the only known method for generating enough productivity to accomplish the megalithic feats of civilization.

A pyramid here, a colosseum there, a gold mine to be excavated, a quarry to be mined, a cathedral to be erected. All of the constructs of civilization, fueled by slaves.

Then came a time when civilization outpaced itself and, in order to expand even further, needed to produce things more quickly than we could even with all the man hours known to man. Human slave labor could not possibly give so much.

It would be absurd to think of powering
a locomotive with a windmill.

We had already begun building grist mills on rivers, harnessing the power of the rushing water to churn our grain much more efficiently than we could. We conceived of mills that harnessed the power of the wind as well.

Yes, the "alternative" energies of today were in fact the first energy sources civilization ever tapped into, thousands of years ago. But windmills and gristmills could never supply enough energy. It would be absurd to think of powering a locomotive with a windmill.

Then we discovered combustion. And fossil fuels.

First there was coal.

Then there was oil.

(Then there wasn't.)

◇

THE WORLD'S FIRST commercial oil well was drilled in

Poland in 1853.

When we really started looking for it, the black gold gushed out of every fissure and well we drilled, and flowed so fast and furious that the best minds of the time couldn't possibly conceive of a future when we would ever come close to using it *all*. (That was also a good half-century before the birth of the modern-day environmentalist movement. So the words 'can' and 'should' were interchangeable. No one considered that there might be any negative environmental effects. Or if anyone did, no one cared.)

The machines we developed and the oil which powered them was a million times more powerful and efficient than human slave labor could ever be.

Today's "alternative" energies were the first sources civilization tapped into, thousands of years ago.

It's no wonder then, that around this exact same time, for the first time in all the known history of humanity, did a global civilization officially abolish slavery. There had always been slave labor. Always.

The American Civil War was a fine thing. The Enlightenment was nice. But neither of these things ended slavery. The discovery of oil as an efficient fuel source did. Anything slaves could do, machines could do better. In the age of Imperialist Economics, if abolition wasn't economically viable, it wouldn't have happened.

◇

ECONOMICS, IN PART, allowed for abolition of slave *labor*.

First there were slave labor.

Then there was coal.

Then there was oil.

(So what happens when there isn't?)

It's a Wonderful Lie

JUST as we erroneously believe that humanity is the end product of evolution—that the world was made for us—Capitalists believe their Holy Corporate Empire is the end product of everything Imperialist Western Culture has been striving to accomplish for the past 6,500 years.

In fact, I suppose it is the end product of what *they've* been trying to accomplish.

Just as our shackles today are not immediately apparent, it isn't obvious how that system will collapse. More of us are waking up today, but a mere half-century ago, no one was the wiser.

The pervasive mindset among the ruling classes for the past seven millennia—world domination, population subjugation and enslavement—has finally manifested the perfect means to its own ends.

The usual methods devised by the ruling classes of previous Empires to control the rabble were cruel and uncivilized.

Primarily, they were:
- Religious oppression required that people believe variations of myths and legends that kept them in trembling fear of God and believing their only hope was attaining Eternal Salvation by following the rules. (The Age of Reason was born in a backlash against religious persecution.)
- Physical Bondage always depended on whips and chains to keep its subjects submissive. (The rise of the Empire of Oil ended all that.)

Under the first two models, slave revolts and heathens had been the plague of civilization. Whenever the quality of life for the masses deteriorated below a critical threshold, uprising and rebellions began.

But today's Holy Corporate Empire need tolerate none of that from their proletariat.

No, no, no, they have created a much more *efficient* system.

◇

WE THE CORPORATIONS, in order to forge more perfect shackles, upon this unshakable premise shall we build our empire: that all slaves are not created equal; that a slave who is unaware of his bondage shall never revolt. Ignorant slaves are willing participants in the very construct designed to oppress them.

As is the plan, the form of slavery that shackles us today is not immediately obvious. It does not involve whips or chains or a life of merciless back-breaking labor. Our lives may not be easy, but we can't realistically compare our lots to those slaves who pushed fifty-ton slabs up Pharaoh's pyramid.

Debt and materialism. Goes together like a
horse and carriage. A match made in Capitalism.

No, our enslavement today is much more elusive, difficult to put your finger on. Like a wisp of smoke, it's there, but it isn't.

Today, we are slaves to debt. And our prison is a materialist culture which we willingly participate in. We are told that through hard-work, we, too can become successful Capitalists (as if that's a good thing).

But we are still building other people's pyramids.

Yes, you say, but look at what we're getting in return for our labor.

We have technology to make our lives easier, mansion-style palaces to dwell in, the likes of which Emperors dared not dream. We posses wonderful, extravagant materialistic things worth a King's ransom that are supposed to make us happier than any generation living before us.

Even the lower classes, the oppressed, impoverished inhabitants of Third World countries, are able to dream of rising through the ranks and achieving the life of a middle-class American. That, they're told and many believe, is something to aspire to.

All in all, it's a wonderful lie.

A great number of us are willing participants in this society, believing wholeheartedly in its benefits. Some of us may think we're being somewhat oppressed, but why dwell on the negatives? We should be thankful! Perhaps banks might run the economy, and tech companies eat all our disposable income, and the health care industry punishes us for getting sick, but, hey, all in all, it's a wonderful lie.

And that is the ultimate manifestation of slavery: when the enslaved believe they are free and work diligently to maintain the very system which oppresses them. Freedom isn't free, we're told.

For it, you have to work for us.

After all these millennia of the ruling class devising new and more inventive methods to manifest their goal of World Domination and enslavement of the masses, the ideal means has finally found expression. Debt and materialism. Goes together like a horse and carriage. A match made in Capitalism.

But there may be light at the end of the tunnel. Even if the masses never wake up from the trance of corporate control, this method of subjugation will prove just as unsustainable as all the rest.

Just as our shackles are not immediately apparent, it also may not be obvious to us all how that system will collapse. I think more of us are waking up to it now, but a mere half-century ago, no one was the wiser.

◇

THE MEANS BY which we are dominated include a paradigm of exponential growth that must always and forever be sustained in order to maintain the illusion. *Exponential growth* and *sustainable* are oxymorons.

That growth is sustained only by our pathological Oedipus complex to devour the world around us. The Empire unabashedly consumes the hand that feeds it, Mother Nature. Soon there will be nothing left to consume.

Then what?

◇

SINCE THE HOLY Corporate Empire is the very epitome of the Western civilization, the end goal, it may prove to be the swan song as well.

The age-old dreams of King Tut, Alexander the Great, Hannibal, Napoleon and Julius Caesar, and a whole host of others will soon finally been realized.

What religious zealots couldn't accomplish with faith, and military generals couldn't take by force, Corporations have accomplished through Capitalism.

They have created the first truly global One World Order. A web of debt has been spun and has ensnared us all.

But the web is about to unravel. There are a million taught strands.

Any one strand could snap at any given time. And when it does, the whole web will begin to unravel.

Then, like Sisyphus, we begin again.

Gross Biospheric Product

ONE PIECE OF evidence that today's world is founded on economics stands head and shoulders above the rest.

In 2010, a French study said precise economic value of the world's rainforests was $5 trillion.

Yes, all the CO_2 the trees absorb, the water they purify, the known medicinal roots, plants, birds, insects, not to mention a few of the world's most powerful neurotoxins found in the skin of poisonous frogs: $5 trillion.

Turns out, all the world's birds, bugs, rivers, oceans,
oil, coal, tar sands, rivers, fish, earth, wind
and fire aren't priceless, after all.

That's not even considering the vast treasure trove of yet-undiscovered pharmaceuticals lurking in the mostly unexplored canopy, just waiting to be plundered by greed. Most conspicuous of all, this "GRP" (Gross Rainforest Product) doesn't factor in that 90% of the rainforest biodiversity is yet to be "discovered."

<>

WOULD YOU BELIEVE IT? As soon as a price tag was put on it, Capitalists started paying more attention to the rainforest.

"What can we do to make it $6 trillion?" they decried in unison.

The idea we can put a price tag on nature is new, but not *that new.* Way back in 1997, the University of Vermont published a study placing the value of the world's *entire biosphere* around $54 trillion ... you know, give or take.

Of course, the study goes on, ecosystem services are not fully 'captured' in commercial markets.

These studies (and there are plenty more) are usually conducted by economic activists (an oxymoron?) trying to convince the rest

of the regular Capitalists that they're being really shortsighted and should stop destroying things.

The brain-children of activists or not, the very notion that the entire value of the biosphere can even be calculated belies the underlying belief that everything (*everything!*) is based on economics.

Turns out, all the world's birds, bugs, rivers, oceans, oil, coal, tar sands, rivers, fish, earth, wind and fire aren't priceless, afterall.

Life as we know it a worth a measly $213 trillion, adjusting for inflation.

◇

BY THE WAY, the Gross Domestic Product of all the human activity in all the countries in the world is only $60 trillion dollars.

The Nomadic Life

NOT all cultures share our obsession with obediently goose-stepping in the parade of progress.

A handful of native tribes have managed to avoid the scourge of the West. And the lives of these tribal people are largely the same today as their parents' parents' parents' parents' lives. They embrace the lifestyle of hunter-gatherers to this day.

Tribes don't wander aimlessly. They share a connection with the land of their ancestors. Settling down to farm would irrevocably change their relationship with the Earth.

"Why don't these people settle down and become farmers?" We ask. "And build towns and villages like *civilized* people? Don't they realize how much better off they'd be if they weren't always wandering from one place to another looking for food?"

When we look at them, we see a people roaming around aimlessly, unsettled nomadic tribes.

They don't see it that way at all. They know they aren't wandering aimlessly. They share a deep connection with the land of their ancestors.

They've chosen not to *settle down* and farm just one small piece of the land because they are connected with everything.

Exploiting one small piece of farmland would irrevocably change their generations' old relationship with the Earth. And not for the better.

These tribes are connected to something intangible. Their roots are deep in their lifestyle. They live their way because it works for them, not because they can't think of a better way.

A PEOPLE'S HISTORY OF CAPITALISM

OUR CULTURE THAT has *settled down* is always and forever on the move, following the path of progress, never knowing where it will lead. While we're waiting to find out, we choose to live in sterile places, prisons. We are inmates of our urban zoos.

Our lives are very different from our parents' lives, even if they grew up in the same city where they raised us.

We live our lives in a constant state of anxiety, as though the world itself is stalking us like some saber-tooth tiger.

We have no connection with any ancestral way of life. In fact, by the time we become old men and women ourselves, we will no longer even have a connection to the lives we lived as young boys and girls. And we will be living in a very alien world.

Though we many live in the same house our entire lives, the world around us continuously becomes unrecognizable.

We can't begin to imagine what world our sons and daughters will end up with. And we're always worried about the future. And we have endless regrets about the past.

Tribesmen may roam throughout the land, but everywhere they travel, they share an intimate knowledge of their world, the Earth. It is the same Earth their ancestors bequeathed them, and will be the same Earth their descendents inherit.

And they don't worry about the future. And they know where their next meal will come from. The land. Always the land.

They are not the nomads. We are.

We are completely uprooted. We wander constantly, with no direction in a forever alien world which we've come to fear. It's a world many of us believe is working against us.

We live our lives in a constant state of anxiety, as though we're being stalked by some saber-tooth tiger in prehistoric times. *It's a dog eat dog world,* we tell ourselves, as if the world itself is stalking us now.

So we end up constantly working to re-imagine our world, always looking for a better life, always searching for new ways to make progress.

Native tribes aren't looking for anything. They've found a way of life that makes them happy. And they hold onto it.

They have natural access to the Utopia we keep trying in vain to invent.

Control, Control, We Must Learn Control

OUR industrialized world of mass produced Capitalism will no doubt have an enduring legacy: pollution, sickness, greed, and the homogenization of all cultures it touches.

But the Industrial Revolution itself may only be the latest in a string of symptoms that's been increasing in severity for thousands of years.

The underlying disease is the mental illness of our race: a pathological need for control. We suffer from a collective obsessive compulsive disorder.

Today, that disorder causes people who believe they are rich to always want more money; and people who believe they are powerful must always consolidate more power.

> Through eccentric rituals, we try to exert
> mind control over the Gods.

The debilitating feeling of being out of control is something we cannot bear to live without.

A lack of control is the underlying root of many addictions, such as drugs or alcoholism. But addictions ultimately result in a person being more out of control; then the addition itself becomes uncontrollable.

◇

WITH EACH NEW invention designed to help us exercise control, we become more addicted to the need for control, and become more and more restless and unhappy and less aware of our inherent unhappiness.

We start mega-dosing on anti-depressants to "cure" depression, which we believe is just an abnormal disease affecting certain individuals.

But depression and anxiety are not just felt on an individual level. They afflict what Carl Jung called our collective consciousness.

As each individual overdoses on their drug of choice (including TV) to anesthetize their individual minds, society as a whole becomes collectively numb to its underlying disorder.

◇

BUT HOW DID we get started down this road in the first place?

The path we've taken seems to trace back to the initial development of some rather bizarre eccentricities.

Way back in the annals of Western Civilization, we started performing eccentric ceremonies to appease the gods, crafting medallions to ward off evil spirits, praying for rain, praying for life, praying to stop floods.

But it was never a desire to *ask* Gods for help, or to *beg* for mercy, that turned us to prayer.

Our prayers and rituals do not assume that God will do what's best for us, if only he knew what we wanted. Our rituals are not intended to communicate our desires to an omnipotent, benevolent God. Our mindset is that God knows what's wrong and lets it happen anyway.

Our rituals, we believe, if carried out successfully, will somehow have power over God—to hypnotize him, make him susceptible to humanities' powers of suggestion.

Through ritual, we desire to control nature into doing what we say. Prayer and ritual is our attempt to exert mind control over God.

This belief—that we can and should be able to control everything, —is truly bizarre.

Even our *desire* to take control over things is mostly absent from the rest of the biosphere of living beings. It's pathological.

It's an obsessive compulsive disorder.

Against the Gods

WE were finally forced to own up to the fact that we couldn't actually exert mind control over God. At which point we decided: Who needs God?

Since God insists he should be in control of our future *(God, what control freak!)* and not allow us to control it ourselves, we decided to just work against God.

In Peter Bernstein's book *Against the Gods: The Remarkable Story of Risk*, the author explains how it was our desire to control our own destiny that ironically made us become so comfortable with taking on tremendous amounts of risk in the stock market.

The stock market is the ultimate manifestation of a society hell-bent on control. We invest in our own financial future, thereby taking fate into our own hands, and out of God's.

Financial certainty, we believe, allows us to live the good life and retire with peace of mind, knowing we are in control of our lives. We have money! We can do anything. We can live as kings. We are in control.

Business forecasting, derivatives and quarterly projections are all designed to manifest the illusion of control over the future.

Making money in the stock market hinges on taking risk. The concept of "Risk Management" says that future risks can be understood, measured and even predicted.

We have become so eccentric, that we think:
1) We can control our fate by making money.
2) We can control risk better than we can control fate.

Thus, born out of a fear of being out of control, we decided to take on a whole lot of risk.

Ironically, to that end, we created the stock market which is by far the most unpredictable thing we've ever invented. Today we are perpetually inventing new strategies to predict, analyze and control the market. And that's even more impossible than controlling fate.

◇

AS AN ASIDE: We even came up with a "security" traded on Wall Street called the VIX. The VIX gains value as fear and uncertainty in the market go up. So, if you're feeling out of control and you think other investors are feeling out of control, too, then invest in the VIX.

The Garden of Earth

WE'VE seen that civilization rose out of our desire to make order out of chaos—to control nature. We've seen that economics rose out of our desire to control the future.

Therefore, Capitalists say, the future of civilization depends on economics.

But the important distinction they miss is that while civilization is based on our need to exert control, economics is only a *derivative* of civilization. Economics is not the fundamental means by which we exercise control, just another means by which we try.

The fundamental way we believe we exercise control—the fundamental thing civilization *is* based on—is agriculture.

Farming was the first ritual we ever created—one which gave us our first illusion of control.

Before trade, before money, before greed, the first thing we thought we could control was our food supply. So we started farming.

But from the very first day we went out into the field, we realized we needed to learn not only to grow the crops we wanted, but also how the keep out the crops that we didn't want.

In controlling our food supply, we also had to learn how to control the weeds. Things got fairly complicated rather quickly.

As it turned out, farming would take much more work, many more hours per day, than the number of hours required to be a successful hunter-gatherer.

Farming was the first ritual we ever created—one which gave us our first illusion of control.

Farming gave us an active role to play in our own lives. It was more work, but it made us feel better, feel as though we were in control. But did it actually put us in control, or just give us the illusion that we were?

It's far more complex to be a successful farmer than a successful hunter-gatherer. Farming is an another example of increasing entropy, a rise in complexity. With each new thing we create in order to exert control over disorder, over nature, to make sense out of chaos, we create an ever increasingly complex, dis-ordered system which we call civilization.

Increasing entropy means more disorder, not more order. It means more to be controlled, *not* more control.

The entropy of the civilized world is no different from the entropy of the universe itself. Both are always increasing.

Since we've recently created artificial man hours through the use of oil-fueled farming machines, we have succeeded in growing so much food that we now play an active role in feeding a population of 7 billion and growing.

There is no better example of increasing entropy than an ever-expanding—and out out-of-control—population.

Today we have become the weeds growing on the garden of Earth. Will we ever learn to control ourselves?

The theory on which civilization was founded is flawed. The idea was that we could control our fate, control our future, and make order from disorder.

Yet for every thing we've ever managed to take under our control, another, more complex thing develops beyond our control.

The stock market started out as a few guys standing on a street corner trading pieces of paper. Look at the complicated, sophisticated, chaotic beast it's developed into today. Vast, incomprehensible, complex.

The entropy of the civilized world is no different from the entropy of the universe itself. Both are always increasing.

A PEOPLE'S HISTORY OF CAPITALISM

Weeds

IMPERIALIST Economics is definitely not the foundation of civilization; it's merely the latest link in a long chain of manifestation of a flawed belief.

If Western civilization is a weed growing in the Garden of Earth, then Imperialist Economics is a weed overrunning civilization like kudzu.

Yet Imperialist Economics is so pervasive that we don't think of it as a weed, but rather as evidence of a booming, bustling, thriving society.

Let's turn our attention to modern American homes, especially suburban homes, those strongholds of successful, upper-crust Capitalists.

We like weeds. We only like weeds. It's why we pick dandelions and cut down the rainforest.

Outside those homes are huge swaths of grass, which their owners call lawns. When a dandelion pops up, we drown it in pesticides, calling it a weed.

But why do we call a dandelion a weed? We can eat dandelions. We can make wine out of dandelions. Dandelions have nutrients people can digest.

People can't eat grass. Sheep and cattle can, but unless you have a petting zoo in your front yard, grass is the real weed. No less than a yacht, grass is a symbol of lavish, irresponsible luxury. Americans spend hours manicuring their weed-patches they call lawns, keeping them meticulously trimmed and free from flowering plants (except flowers of their choosing, which they purchase from *the store.*)

An obsessively maintained, flourishing lawn is evidence of an affluent upper-Middle Class homeowner. The biggest, best maintained ones are often found in the suburbs of America.

We like weeds. We only like weeds. We have a love affair with weeds. It's why we pick dandelions. It's why we cut down the rainforest and re-plant the soil with poisonous crops like tobacco.

We are seeding the world with weeds.

Why wouldn't we? We ourselves are weeds.

And we're fruitful and multiplying.

Corporate Weeds

WHEREVER local communities have begun building stronger local economies, corporate American weeds begin to pop up.

It's an alarming trend, a backlash against the move towards independent, locally-based economies happening in many communities across America. Independent-minded towns and cities have begun to notice that cultivating a strong local economic base is a very successful strategy for making their local community "recession-proof."

Certain grocery stores, banks and magazines
are wolves in sheep's clothing.

In communities where more money is kept in circulation locally, economies remain strong, and have lower unemployment rates.

But when locally earned money is spent in corporate stores, the money disappears into a black hole of deep pockets, never to be seen again.

Communities have started to notice that.

And corporate America has noticed that we've noticed. And found a way to exploit it.

Watch out, they're popping up like weeds.

◇

So HOW THE heck can national corporations wedge their way into local communities specifically trying to stop them from doing just that?

It started (where else?) with banks. Certain local community banks started joining together with local community banks from other, far away communities under a national umbrella, with the idea of pooling their money into a centralized agency (who would then invest that pool in the stock market.)

Immediately, this meant that local banks were now participating in the con to funnel money away from the local level.

Money can't be created or destroyed.
It simply changes hands.

"No, no, no!" they defended their motivations, "We're using the money to create more money to give back to the local community."

Rubbish. Creating more money out of thin air devalues all of the money, everywhere. It is impossible to give back more money than the amount of value lost in the process.

Money can't be created or destroyed. It simply changes hands.

The end game is to transform all previously local banks into one big national bank, with locally owned branches.

Call it the National Bank of Small Town America, or the innocent sounding Financial Co-op of America. But don't be fooled. This is a corporate weed growing in a local garden.

This is not a the Financial Co-op. It's a Financial Coup.

◇

IT STARTED WITH banks, but that was just the beginning.

The local movement was catching on, and what better way to tap into a new trend than to publish national magazines that cater to an emerging trend of buying local.

Chicago's Conscious Community; Charlott's Conscious Community; California's Conscious Community. (Your town or state doesn't have to start with a 'C' to participate.)

All of these locally-branded magazines give the appearance of being locally run, but are merely wearing corporate camouflage and infiltrating local movements.

The spirit of the local movement demands that businesses be locally owned and operated, *none* of the profits nationalized, and more than anything, *Independent*. A franchise doesn't qualify.

These magazines (and banks) are just that: locally-owned franchises of a national corporation. At least half of the cash flow becomes corporate backwash, and in the case of the magazines, more than half of the content is syndicated.

These grocery stores, banks and magazines are
wolves in sheep's clothing. Don't be fooled. They'll
huff and they'll puff and they'll blow your economy down.

Who else is getting in on the game? National Health Food stores trying to exploit the 'buy locally-grown, fresh produce' trend.

Whole Foods Market has re-branded itself in its own image in certain communities it's infiltrated.

It gives itself a unique name (Green Life Grocery) which it hopes gives the impression that it's a local, independent store.

It is not. In fact, these re-branded stores aren't even locally owned franchises. They're corporate through-and-through.

Green Life then places ads in the locally syndicated magazines I mentioned earlier and banks with the Financial Coup (excuse me, Co-op).

These grocery stores, banks and magazines are wolves in sheep's clothing. Don't be fooled. They'll huff and they'll puff and they'll blow your economy down.

C-SUITE

CORPORATIONS are bad. Financial Corporations are worse. But when otherwise-honest corporations who make products start playing the financial game too, that's by far the most destructive incarnation of greed.

Wealthy investors today are buying up whole fleets of companies that used to be direct competitors.

These investors cherry-pick companies not on the basis of the products they make, but on the basis of how lucrative their industry is, and how many competitors they have—and how good at making money they are.

The members of a Corporate C-Suite are like the serpents on Medusa's head. You know the CEO, the CFO, the CIO, and the E-I-E-I-O. But do you know the most dangerous C-Suite position of all?

There is one sole objective in doing this, and it's not to continue making the product these companies have manufactured for generations.

The end goal is to make money.

Huge corporate conglomerates, even monopolies, are sheltered under a single investors' umbrella.

The fat is trimmed, redundancies are eliminated, 1/3 or more of the all the production facilities are shut down and as many employees as possible are let go.

One or two of the individual entities may be intentionally run into the ground over a few short years—or dissolved in order to sell off its various departments.

The shadowy investors at the top, masterminding the whole

charade, outrank the CFOs and CEOs and the 49% of all other corporate shareholders.

These ultra-wealthy investors are a new addition to the long line of "C-Suite" executives affectionately known as "job creators" we've all come to know and love.

The members of a corporate C-Suite are like the serpents on Medusa's head. You know the CEO, the CFO, the CIO and the E-I-E-I-O. But do you know the most dangerous C-Suite position of all?

The head of the snake is the multi-billion dollar trans-national investors. That's the CCO.

The Chief Capitalist Officer.

The Green Counter-Revolution

SINCE 1990, the market for organic products has grown from nothing to $55 billion in 2009 according to Organic Monitor (www.organicmonitor.com).

When conservative-Capitalists sneer at this revolution, they juxtapose organic farming with what they call "traditional" agricultural practices. (By which they mean hybridized seeds, synthetic fertilizers, and pesticides.)

There's nothing "traditional" about any of that. Chemical companies growing our food is a *tradition* that only dates back to World War II.

Organic farming is a *counter*-revolution.

On the behest of the U.S. government, American chemical companies produced neural-toxins for the war against Nazis. When there were no more Nazis, they had to find something else to do with all those chemicals. On the behest of Capitalists, chemical companies found out that diluting their neural-toxins yielded pesticides which the world had never seen before.

What today is a just a "trend" towards organic farming that's luckily been catching on, had been the only way to grow crops for the past 10,000 years. Today we think of the move towards organic as "A Green Revolution."

Sorry, that term's already been taken, monopolized by Capitalists since the 1960s. Ironically, the original term "Green Revolution" refers to the very thing that organic farming is fighting against! Organic farming is not a revolution but a counter-revolution.

GREEN CAN MEAN many things—only one of which is anything good. Don't be deceived. There was nothing "green" about the "Green Revolution" except the money it made.

Norman Borlaug was equal parts humanitarian and the Dr. Frankenstein of agriculture. While his motivations were pure, he never anticipated the consequences of his actions.

The original term "Green Revolution" refers to a series of research, development, and technology transfer initiatives beginning after World War II that increased agriculture production around the world by introducing hybridized seeds, synthetic fertilizers, and pesticides for the first time.

The term "Green Revolution" was first used in 1968 by former United States Agency for International Development (USAID) director William Gaud, who noted the spread of the new technologies and said, "These and other developments in the field of agriculture contain the makings of a new revolution. It is not a violent Red Revolution like that of the Soviets, nor is it a White Revolution like that of the Shah of Iran. I call it the Green Revolution."

The wide-spread usage of the new farming techniques found a staunch advocate in Norman Borlaug, who was equal parts humanitarian and the Dr. Frankenstein of agriculture. While his motivations were pure, he never anticipated the consequences of his actions.

Today, our history book bestow upon him the title "Father of the Green Revolution" and credit him with saving over a billion people from starvation by Frankenstein-izing farming techniques.

Yet since his Green Revolution began, world population has grown from 2.5 billion in 1950 to 7 billion in 2011.

The proportion of people living in the developing world of

Africa, Asia, and Latin America and the Caribbean has expanded from 68 percent to more than 80 percent of the total.

The Third World is where all those billion people Borlaug saved from starvation live.

So if we're going to Norman Borlaug for saving a billion lives, we must also remember to credit him with giving the world 4.5 billion more mouths to feed.

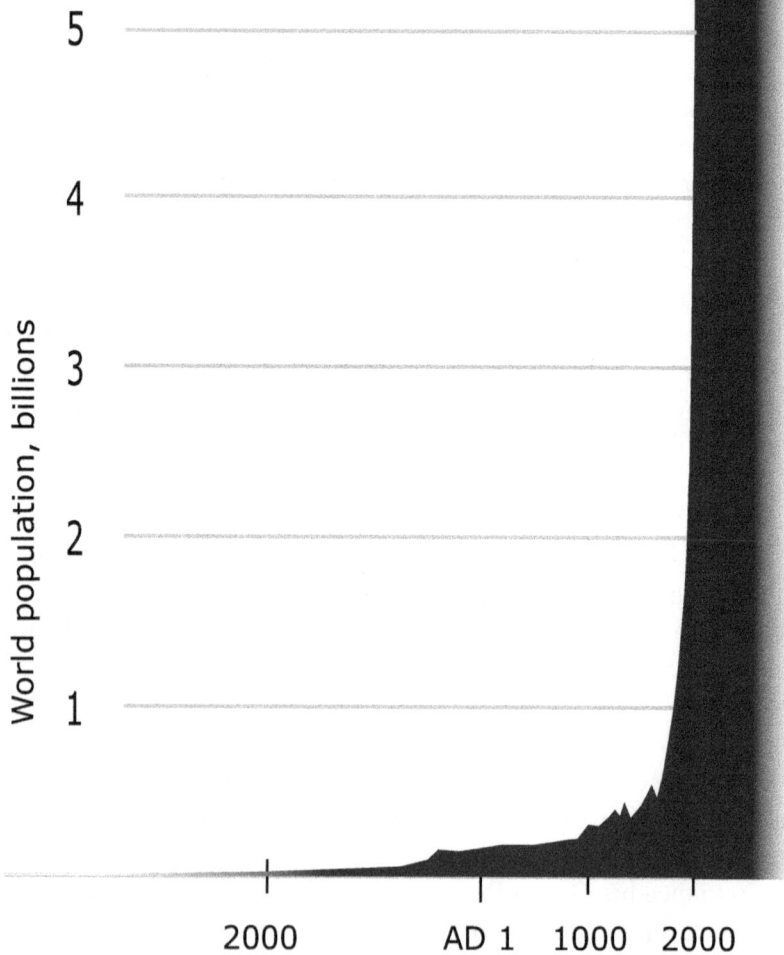

World population, billions

7

6

5

4

3

2

1

2000   AD 1   1000   2000

Source: Wikipedia commons

A SŌSTAINABLE SCAM

IN some of its practice, but certainly not in principle, sustainable agriculture has turned to the dark side of Capitalism.

The larger the "fair-trade" label, the more suspicious you might want to be. Companies have realized they can use this marketing strategy to convince "green-minded" people to pay a lot of money (more than fair-value.) We've all been drinking the corporate Kool-Aid which tells us that fair-trade is only a sustainable practice if the end product carries a hefty price tag.

How did non-organic farming come to be known as "traditional" agriculture? Chemical companies growing our food is a tradition that only dates back about 50 years.

My favorite Health Food Market chain (to point the finger at) places organic products on its shelves right next to their traditional-Capitalist counterparts, the former carrying a price tag 2-3 times higher.

I can almost hear the twisted logic echoing from the other side of the political grocery aisle. "You want organic? Fine. This is Capitalist America after all! If there's a demand for it, we'll find a way to supply it. But it's not going to be cheap! You realize, don't you, that since you're making us grow your liberal foods without fertilizers or pesticides, the land is only going to be like 1/5 as productive. That's land we could be using to feed starving children in Africa! But if you liberals want organic, you got it! As long as you realize you're killing African babies! Baby-killers! No, actually, ho! ho! we don't care about the babies! We're Capitalists! As long as you're willing to pay for all the land you're hoarding with your selfish need for organic, green produce, we'll sell it to you! Sure!"

Don't you believe any of it for one second! It's rubbish!

Time and again, green-minded people do choose to pay an exorbitant premium for organic foods. I don't think any of us really believes we're killing babies by buying organic. Then again on some level, maybe we do.

We believe organic is worth a huge premium, so we must believe that it's more expensive to produce. We believe farmland that isn't spayed, neutered and artificially inseminated is less productive. And if we believe that, then the killing babies argument rings true—we could be growing more food to feed more people.

But don't worry. That's not true either.

If anything, the price structure for organic versus non-organic should be flip flopped. So why aren't they?

All those pesticides we spray on fields, like everything else we do, simply creates more entropy. Pesticides to kill one bug require fertilizers to protect the soil against the pesticides, and so on. Buying all those chemicals far outweighs the monetary cost of organic farming. And, with all those pesticides, the land becomes less productive, not more, as is "traditionally" thought. And the produce yielded by chemically-treated soil has far fewer nutrients.

Pesticides, herbicides and fertilizers equals more expensive farming techniques, less nutritious food, less productive land.

Organic equals less expensive farming techniques, more productive land, more nutritious food.

If anything, the price structure for organic versus non-organic should be flip flopped. So why aren't they? Because cereal-Capitalists (or should I say serial-Capitalists) are making a killing in the grocery business when they sell "organic." They don't only meet the "green" need. They exploit it.

A PEOPLE'S HISTORY OF CAPITALISM

They see green-minded consumers as fanatic environmentalists who will pay anything for sustainable farming and healthy food.

We have unwittingly supplied the Capitalists a method for achieving much fatter "organic" profit margins.

Are Greenies really as naive as Capitalists think? Do we really pay exorbitant premiums because we're that gullible?

Perhaps in part.

But I think there's another reason we willingly shell out $5/lb for organic oranges. (If you're reading this ten years down the road and across the other side of hyper-inflation, let me assure you, $5/lb for oranges is an absurd price in 2011).

So why *do* we pay it?

A RAW DEAL

RAW food restaurants have recently burst onto the culinary scene, and they are getting away with the same price gouging as our favorite Health Food Market.

In defense of raw food "chefs," (a chef who doesn't cook? We need another name for these people) they are arguably buying all their ingredients from the Capitalists who run the grocery stores, so they may actually need to charge exorbitant prices. Maybe.

But why the heck are people willing to pay $50 for an elaborately prepared "raw" lunch? Can't we just toss a salad at home?

No sane person would pay $50 for lunch. Someday, with inflation. But not today! Not yet! (Or maybe today if you work on Wall Street ...but, no, then you're a pathological Capitalist and you don't count in the sane category anyway.)

There is no need for unreasonably
inflated prices. Except Capitalism.

And yet otherwise rational, middle-of-the-road people *are* paying $50 for a raw lunch everyday. For one key reason.

Guilt.

Guilt over consuming fast food and GM grocery "foodstuffs" has been eating at them for years, if not decades. Today, a few of us have finally woken up to high fructose corn syrup and all the rest. And finally, now that there is a raw food option, which can purportedly *cleanse* your body, a few of us (out of the few of us) are falling head over heals for it.

It's cathartic. Like seeing a food psychiatrist. (Can we call raw a food chefs a Foochiatrists? Foo-foo-ychiatrist?)

Sane people really won't pay—and aren't paying—$50 for lunch.

They're paying $50 for absolution. They're paying to feel empowered to do something about their otherwise bad eating habits.

Paying to gain a sense of *control* over the problem.

◇

WHETHER IT'S THE obnoxious in-your-face image of fair-trade/organic/sustainable that ceremoniously proclaims "Healthy! Good for the Planet!" or promises of a "raw food cleanse," both fulfill a need. They convince us we're doing a good deed, good for the planet, good for ourselves, and that finally, we're able to do something about a problem that's been out of our hands for far too long. Finally, we might be able to bring it under control. And we don't care what that costs.

But family farmers will tell you that growing organic is in fact less expensive than growing "by traditional means." And as long as they practice crop rotation, organic practices are completely sustainable.

There is no need for these unreasonably inflated prices.

Except Capitalism.

◇

I RECENTLY MET a local part-time urban farmer who raises chickens and sells local, organic eggs to her neighbors. Way to go, right? That's building a local community!

Alas, no.

She sells her eggs for $5/dozen!

> As she proudly defended her own practice of price gouging, she railed about the cost of gas out of the other side of her mouth.

"If someone doesn't want to pay $5, there's always someone else who will. So why should I sell them for less than the top dollar someone's willing to pay?"

She quite proudly proclaimed her egg-selling philosophy as I toured her urban garden. Then she complained about the price of gas in her next breath and the ungodly amount of money she had to shell out for her hybrid car.

She also told us that her husband calls her an egg Nazi.

I think what he means is that gouging people for eggs is unfair, immoral. I think most of us would agree with him.

So he calls her a Nazi. That's kind of our generic word for someone who is cruel or unjust or immoral or whatever.

It's kind of a knee-jerk reaction we all have. Don't agree with a person's outlook? Call them a Nazi or a socialist or a communist or something else.

But gouging people for eggs isn't the behavior of a Nazi.

What he means to call her is a Capitalist.

A PEOPLE'S HISTORY OF CAPITALISM

A FAIR TRADE?

NOT only are the signs proclaiming "organic" "sustainable" and "fair trade" a marketing gimmick, the actual practice of "fair trade" itself is often fairer for corporations than farmers.

My beloved national Health Food Market claims it pays fair-trade farmers fair-value. As long as that value is calculated in the farmers' local Second- or Third World currency.

And that's a pittance when calculated in American Dollars—the currency the products will be resold for.

The corporate scheme to convert all value disparity to pure profit proliferates the transfer of wealth to the top and creates a top-heavy world economy, not a flat one.

So the corporations may pay farmers eight bolivar, escudos, pesos, pesetas etc., for fair-trade produce instead of two pesos. That doesn't hardly matter when there are something like 1,500 bolivar, escudos, pesos, pesetas etc., to the dollar, and the same produce will be resold in the U.S. for, say, $5.

The lion's share of that $5 goes to pad corporate pockets.

Now, in defense of corporate profits—wait, no, there is no defense for corporate profits.

In defense of Capitalist swindlers (yeah, that's better) who claim, that if they were to pay local farmers fair-value as priced in U.S. Dollars, the disparity would completely topple the local economy. Neither can that same crop be re-sold in the U.S. for 2¢ for the same reason.

All of that's true enough. Nevertheless, in "fair-trade," it's considered fair-game to make a killing in the currency trade.

You see, the corporations declare, we really are stuck between a rock and a hard place! And the only way out is to pocket the money in the middle!

Oh, poor, poor corporate America. Their "solution" to convert the value disparity to profit proliferates the transfer of wealth to the top and creates a top-heavy world economy.

◇

THIS CLEARLY DISPELS the illusion of a "Flat World" economy promoted by economist Thomas Freedman.

The concept of the flat earth says that in our global economy, it makes no difference where work is done or products are produced since all the economies of the world are interdependent.

The belief in this argument has helped fuel the corporate-sponsored rise of "free-trade" agreements, which prohibits governments from levying export and import tariffs.

Once upon a time, the money left over in the middle was taxed by governments of the world, and thus, returned to the People.

Governments and people all over the world have been hoodwinked into believing that tariffs unfairly cut into corporate profits, and prevent corporations from doing their job as "job creators."

That's absolute nonsense.

Once upon a time, the money left over in the middle was taxed by the governments of the world, and thus, returned to the People through investments in the commons, such as bridges, roads, sewage and sanitation. Of course, that assumes the government isn't completely corrupt by Wall Street. It is, no doubt, somewhat—maybe even mostly—corrupt, so a large percentage of the money in the middle, if taxed, may get sucked into a black hole of corporate oil wars and all the rest anyway.

But when the money in the middle is not taxed, it's guaranteed to get sucked into the black hole on Wall Street.

The Edge of the Flat World

THROUGH the belief in a "Flat World" economy, "fair-trade" is corrupted into "free-trade"—which means tax-free for corporations.

In order for the global economy not to fall off the edge of Friedman's Earth, the price of labor and the cost of goods everywhere would have to be uniform. And even then we'd be treading in dangerous waters. Look at the trouble in the flat world of the Eurozone. When the water gets choppy, ripples hit every shoreline.

◇

THE FLAT EARTH concept is just another weapon in the corporate arsenal to bankrupt the governments of the world, thereby eliminating them from the picture all together.

To add insult to injury, the eight bolivar, escudos, pesos, pesetas etc., which free trade brings to local farmers are not always freely given. Oh, no, the puppet masters have plenty of strings attached.

Materialism manifests and Capitalism spreads.
More hamsters run on the treadmill of Capitalism.
That's the "free-trade" 10-step program in a nutshell.

They set conditions whereby local farmers are "encouraged" to "re-invest" six of their bolivar, escudos, pesos, pesetas etc., in their own infrastructure. That seems on the surface to be a good thing, except the end game is to develop inroads for American corporate markets.

The local farmers, in using their wages to build up their own industrial infrastructure, become unwitting pawns in the corporate harvest of ever-more efficiently produced crops. And that means the low price they already pay for Second- and Third World crops becomes subsidized by the very money they're using to buy the crops in the first place.

Though volume has increased—and in aggregate more money is flowing into local economies—the people there are also working harder than ever before to make all that extra money. They become hamsters on the treadmill of Capitalism. Is that a fair trade?

As more money flows into the community, other American corporations salivate over a new market, and they swoop in to give the locals plenty of options on how to spend their new-found wealth.

Materialism manifests and Capitalism spreads.

That's the "free-trade" 10-step program in a nutshell.

I'm sure corporate language for it is a lot more eloquent than mine. Their language probably utilizes their favorite buzz words, "identifying emerging markets" and "investing in local economies."

◇

NOW I'M NOT arguing that these Second- and Third World countries should be left in the Dark Ages of poverty.

But, as we'll see, Second- and Third World countries are a creation of the very corporations who now position themselves as the salvation of the poor and impoverished.

"Probably the greatest weapon of mass destruction
is corporate economic globalization."

—Kenny Ausubel

PART 4

Crimes Against Humanity

Stereotypical
Economic Stereotyping

THE distinctions of First, Second, and Third World which have come to stereotype all of the known world are today primarily economic in nature. (Everything is, remember?)

Classifying everything into a hierarchy has been the obsession of Western Culture since the 1800s when the modern "scientific method" was born. This methodology (or should I say mythology?) for understanding the world bleaches the whole living Earth into a hierarchical system of sterile phylum, genus, class, kingdom, domain, and order.

These biological classifications are known as "taxonomic" ranks. *Tax-onomic.* I'm not kidding. We think everything, (literally *everything*) is primarily economic in nature.

Just because our own Western Civilization was built up (and breaks down) hierarchically, why do we automatically assume that all of Life follows a "natural" organizational hierarchy? Projecting a bit are we?

It's no surprise that we use a stereotypical stereotype for classifying all of human civilization into three hierarchical categories: The First-, Second-, and Third- World.

◇

JUST AS A matter of curiosity, it might come as a surprise to you that the terms First, Second, and Third World were not initially economic distinctions. They originated during the Cold War as a way to categorize countries that either had nuclear capabilities, were developing a nuclear program, or posed no threat to the "developed" world at all.

Journey to the
Middle ("Second") World

THE South American country of Ecuador today has been consumed by its stereotypical designation as a "second-world" country. Ecuador is now best known as a testament to Spanish colonialism.

The tiny country lies on the West Coast of South America, smack dab in the middle of the world. Not only does Ecuador find itself in the middle of our hierarchical system of classifying countries, its capital city, Quito, also lies smack dab on the equator. The literal middle of the world.

Quito is considered the cultural capital of
South America. Ironically, very little of its
thousand-year old culture remains.

Quito actually means "middle land," in the language of the Quitus people, who founded the city at the gravitational center of the Earth c. 980 AD. They pinpointed the precise location of the Earth's equator 1,000 years before the Europeans, and with a much greater degree of accuracy. In 1735, a French expedition proudly proclaimed it had "discovered" the Center of the Earth … in fact misplacing the equator by more than 600 feet.

The city of Quito is not only the capital of Ecuador, but it's also considered the cultural capital of South America. Ironically, very little of its thousand-year old culture remains. Spanish colonial architecture dominates the city's "historic" district. Today Catholic churches built a few short centuries ago pockmark the city, as if to rub salt in the fatal wound to the rich variety of dead religions, ancient beliefs, and time-honored customs that today are all but extinct.

◇

THE ANCIENT CULTURES of Ecuador date back 5,500 years, likely to the dawn of the Valdivia Culture, the oldest recorded civilization in the Americas.

Modern descendents of the Valdivia Culture include a tribe which Spanish Conquistadores characterized as the Amazonian head-hunters.

They lopped off as many Western heads as they could in the first few centuries of invasion, earning their reputation.

Legend has since turned them into cannibals, which they are not. Sounds like Western Culture, which is devouring their ancestral homeland in the Amazon Rainforest and ravishing the land for oil, is projecting again.

Western armies proudly wave the green flag
of Capitalism as we triumphantly march into
battle in our War against Mother Nature.

The real people behind these legendary peoples are two distinct groups of what we Westerners like to call "non-contact" people.

They are known as the Tagaeri and the Taromenani (families) of the Huaorani (tribe).

In total, their number has dwindled to several hundred, from a civilization that was once well over a million.

Through their stalwart perseverance, and across a 300-year timeline of Western influence, starting with the Spanish Conquistadores, and today morphing into the Oil Tycoon-adores, the Huaorani have managed to defend their lands against any unwanted contact with the West. To a man, they will gladly sacrifice themselves to defend their lifestyle for their children's children.

The Huaorani have become known in recent decades for their

guerilla raids on oil fields in the jungle. Wielding eight-foot long blowpipes nocked with poison arrowheads, and able to scale giant Kapok trees with the stealth of jaguars, the Huaorani materialize from the shadows, killing mercilessly and destroying everything and everyone of the West who comes into contact with them or accidently strays into their territory. They do so in self-defense.

All of their brethren have long since been conquered and now wear t-shirts and jeans from Banana Republic and wonder, as they watch re-runs of Gilligan's Island, "Can't our brothers and sisters see what civilization can do for them?"

Why, yes, they can, actually. They see oil fires consuming their lands, rampant deforestation threatening their millennia-old lifestyle as Western armies proudly wave the green flag of Capitalism amd triumphantly march into battle in our War against mother nature.

The Napo River is the frontline in one of many ongoing battles. The river runs the length of Ecuador, supplying water and transportation to native villagers just as it has for thousands of years. Flowing south, it will eventually converge with another river and form the Amazon.

Oil fields line the Napo shoreline in Ecuador. A few hundred Huaorani with spears? Ha! This is where oil companies don't fear to tread.

Crude is extracted there, along with its "by-product," natural gas.

While the crude is exported, no one wants the natural gas. What a burden! The logistics of capturing it and transporting it would never make a dime. So what to do with this pesky problem?

Here, wanton wastefulness converges with greed, and their offspring is anything but pretty.

> This is where oil companies don't fear to tread.
> For a few million dollars profit, they would destroy
> all of it without a second thought.

The unwanted natural gas is siphoned skyward from the well through a long metal pipe where it is consumed in an eternal flame burning day and night.

Imagine the space shuttle blasting off from Cape Canaveral and you get a pretty clear idea what the flame billowing out the top of this metal siphon sounds like in contrast with the absolute stillness of the jungle.

The fire will burn continuously for at least five years. Villagers living nearby suffer headaches, fatigue, and a host of other chronic ailments, both physical and psychological—never mind the gross malfeasance of the whole thing.

Yet as the oil companies see it, all this is a small price to pay.

At night, looking out on inky black skies overhead, there's a unique sort of light pollution shimmering on the horizon.

On a country road leading into any major city in the U.S., you're sure to see a solid orange wall rising into the night sky, fortifying all our cities from being invaded by the forces of darkness. But on the Ecuadorian horizon, there wasn't a solid wall, but a shimmering light, pulsing like a candle in a dark room, far, far away from the nearest electrically-lit human settlement.

This was the aggregate light from a hundred such flames as the one I saw first-hand burning on the Napo River river. Colossal oil fields scar the Earth on land that was primary rainforest not twenty years ago.

We worry about crimes against humanity.
This is a corporate crime wave against Ecology.

For a few million dollars profit, Capitalists would destroy all of it without a second thought. Well, they might have given it a second thought when the French study came out in 2010, estimating the value of the rainforest at a few trillion dollars a year.

We worry about crimes against humanity. This is a corporate crime wave against Ecology. If you ever have a chance to step into even the smallest pocket of what's left of the primordial jungle, with one breath of air, one flash of insight, you will experience for yourself a deeper, richer, more vibrant world than anything you have ever known, and a more personal, gut-wrenching, intimate sense of the pathological nature of corporate crime.

The Economics of Paradise:
A Global Climate Change

SILKY wisps of moonlight filter like strands of a spider's web through the canopy of one of the world's most remote rainforests. Among the dense foliage where the silver vines of moonlight are denied purchase lurk lemurs known as Indri. Trying to get a nocturnal glimpse of the Indri is one of the island of Madagascar's most unique tourist attractions. This untamed rainforest, called Andasibe, is the only place on the planet the endangered species can be found.

Suddenly, a cacophony erupts in the jungle. The Indri screech like sirens. Something has frightened them.

> 90% of the species on Madagascar are endemic.
> 85% of their forested habitat has been lost
> to slash-and-burning.

You'd need to be a few miles away to see what only the Indri can from their hundred-foot high home in the canopy: a sharp ridge of orange fire cutting through the darkness, devouring another half-dozen hectares of rainforest on the other side of the park. This is slash-and-burn deforestation, and it's rampant throughout most of the countryside.

Madagascar is the fourth largest island in the world and one of the most remote places on the planet, located off the southeastern coast of Africa. It has all the trappings of a tropical paradise and is a growing hotspot for ecotourism. It's easy to see why. The island boasts some of the deepest and most remote rainforests on the planet and some of the world's most unique wildlife.

IN HIS BOOK *The Eighth Continent,* Peter Tyson describes Madagascar as a "living laboratory." Nearly 90% of the species on Madagascar are endemic to the island. Of course 85% of their forested habitat has already been lost to aggressive (and highly ineffective) slash-and-burn agricultural techniques.

While the island is one of the ecologically richest countries in the world, according to the International Conservation Committee, it also ranks among the "top" ten poorest. It is firmly entrenched in the Third World.

For all our bravado about helping locals achieve a higher standard of living, our real motives are obvious: to groom a market for American consumerism.

For their part, the tropical hotspots on Madagascar are some of the world's little known treasures. Fueled by tourism dollars brought in by national state parks like Andasibe and tropical beaches, the rapidly growing industry of ecotourism in Madagascar may hold the only hope for strengthening the economy.

The economy limps along, desperately trying to be something it is not: a world suited to being grafted with Western Economics.

Before the West arrived, people there were doing just fine.

Forcing it to conform to a system of Western Capitalism is having predictable results: inequitable wealth distribution, famine, poverty, and a class of Capitalist oppressors.

Hmmm... come to think of it, can't the same be said for the entire world?

Indeed, the West suffers from a serious case of bi-polar disorder. This is in evidence on Madagarcar where the two biggest industries, eco-tourism and rainforest destruction are like oil and water.

With only 15% of the island's original forest cover remaining (cut down in the name of profit), there will soon come a time

A PEOPLE'S HISTORY OF CAPITALISM

when there's not much left for tourists to see.

But for the time being, Madagascar is open for business.

Occupation lasted some 65 years, bringing with it
industry, technology, wealth for the colonizers,
paved roads, oppression and deforestation.

Governmental programs and NGOs alike are carving inroads, teaching English to the locals, and "modern," more productive agricultural techniques. Yet for all their bravado about helping the locals achieve a higher standard of living, their real motives are obvious: groom markets for American consumerism.

◇

THE GLOBALIZATION OF Madagascar began as early as the 1500s, when the island was "discovered" by the European nation of Portugal. Christian missionaries were soon to follow. Think they were invited? What goes around comes around, and France soon honed in on Portugals's territory, just as the Portugese had finished subduing any Malagasy resistance to Westernization and Catholacism. Madagascar was declared a French colony in 1896. Its occupation lasted some 65 years, and brought with it industry, technology, wealth to the colonizers, paved roads, oppression and deforestation.

And then, in 1960, when the political climate of the western world no longer favored, or profited from, imperialism, the French simply picked up and left.

A souvenir T-shirt costs US $20, enough to feed a family
for a month. The families see none of the money.
That's the economics of a tourist paradise.

As terrible as the flood of poverty that washed over the land in the wake of the French pull-out, it was what the French left behind that caused the most significant devastation.

They'd transformed the climate from a peaceful, prosperous agrarian society into one infected by the Western plague of Greed.

An upper class of Malagasy emerged, eager to fill the post the French had recently abandoned. The Malagasy people no longer needed the West to oppress them. They were now capable of doing it themselves.

Teach a man how to fish and all that.

◇

FIFTY MILES EAST of the capital of Antanaravio lies the small town of Mantasoa. Under French control, Mantasoa was the industrial capital of the country. What's left today is a ruin, whose staple crops are rice and bananas, never yielding enough to feed the population.

Today there are annual famines in the south of Madagascar, when even rice (their country's staple crop) becomes scarce.

The vanilla bean is Madagascar's top export. When Vanilla Coke was first introduced, Madagascar became the top supplier of vanilla to the Coca-Cola Company. But the company found other distributors when the Malagasy government collapsed in 2002, and never returned its business even after the peaceful establishment of the new government.

> Madagascar limps along, desperately trying to be something it is not: a world suited to being grafted with a Western Economy.

Madagascar has one of the lowest GDPs of any country. The nutrient-rich rice they farm is exported for profit. Nutrient blanched white rice is imported to feed the people.

Aggressive slash-and-burn agricultural technique is ultimately self-defeating as a means of clearing more usable land for sustainable farming, but a very effective way of producing a windfall of cash for up to five seasons of rice growing before all the nutrients are depleted from the soil. After the windfall ends, the landslide begins, and the island bleeds red, eroded soil into the ocean. The "bleeding" island can be seen from orbit.

◇

So what's left to fuel the economy? Things have come much too far to easily revert back to the previous way of life, before the French.

Madagascar's best hope for economic salvation lies in the country's newly burgeoning eco-tourism industry—the same industry that's being threatened by slash-and-burning.

> Colonization has transformed the climate
> from a peaceful, prosperous agrarian society
> into one infected by the Western plague of Greed.

Ironically, tourists come mainly from France, Madagascar's ex-colonials, though anti-French sentiment lingers in the cultural memory of the Malagasy.

And eco-tourism isn't good for everybody.

One recently established state park, Ranomafana, came at the cost of denying 27,000 of the poorest people in the world access to subsistence resources.

In other words, so that Frenchmen could bask in the sun and look at Lemurs, the local people were booted off their land and denied access to natural resources they had been using sustainably since time out of memory.

But it's the lesser of two evils. Had the conservation societies not stolen the land, the Oil Companies were lining up to take it.

For my part, I have seen first-hand just how the Malagasy people live on the periphery of such national parks as Ranomafana. The poverty is heartbreaking.

This is a tourist paradise, but a local nightmare. These are the poorest people in the world.

In Andasibe state park, where we saw the endangered Indri lemurs screaming in the night, a souvenir T-shirt emblazoned with a hand-stitched Indri costs US $20—or, enough to feed a whole family for a month. The families don't get that money, of course.

That's the economics of paradise.

Why Poverty is Politically Correct

So we've just seen the Second- and Third Worlds, though our brief stops there only scratch the surface.

I've traveled between the worlds, lived with a host family in Madagascar and spent time in rural villages in Africa and South America.

Through cultural immersion, I was able to learn something of the way of life there, but at best it was an approximation of those peoples' realities.

In our posh First World surroundings, we are showered with technological obsessions, adorned in avarice, swaddled in comfort, lavished with luxuries beyond the wildest dreams of decadence of all generations of humanity before us.

Capitalism causes poverty.

Few of us will ever truly come to know a life other than the one we were born into. Most of us wouldn't have the stomach for it.

Suffice it to say that there are three ways to live human life on the planet Earth at this moment in history.

1) The way the Kings of Capitalism live.

2) The way its victims live.

3) The way humans lived for the 70,000 years before Western Civilization ever came to be.

◇

IF YOU LEARN Western history the way it's taught in the West or study sociology from a Western Imperialist perspective, there's one set of questions that's hardly ever addressed. In fact, our schoolbooks steer our minds away from even asking.

The question is, why is there so much poverty in the world? Why is there a "Third World?" Why are we so rich and the rest of the world so poor? And how did it come to be this way?

We think, today, that we are no longer beholden to the racist views that predominated the Western mindset a mere 2-3 generations ago. Then, it was believed we were simply superior, and the rest of humanity was simply inferior. It wasn't *civilized*. Other peoples were *barbaric*.

And why was this the case? 2-3 generations ago, the answer was easy. "Gods made us superior." God simply made it our place to civilize the heathens.

Today, some of us know better.

Others like to think they know better, but still act as though they don't.

◇

WHEN WE BELIEVED in the "Inferiority of Species," we had very cut and dry answer to the question of, "Why is there poverty?"

Ask people today and they'll probably stare at you blankly. Their grandparents would have said "God made us superior."

While we might have abandoned our grandparents' belief, now we find ourselves in a kind of head-scratching limbo.

It's as if it's a blind spot in the Western world view. A blind spot we don't even see.

Poverty is the politically correct term for oppression.

Perhaps some of us have just never considered the question in our lifetimes. We all *know* poverty exists. We see infomercials about it all the time. We're encouraged to donate money to humanitarian aid.

We're encouraged to pity poverty just enough that we feel guilt. We feel just enough guilt to give money to charity in order to help make the most visible symptom of poverty (hunger) disappear. We're not encouraged to ask, "Why?" only "What can I do?"

We're not encouraged to connect the dots.

Although we claim to no longer believe it was God's plan for us to save the world, we're still doing just that. Only now it's done under the guise of humanitarian aid, not colonialism.

But aren't we doing the same thing?

One hundred years after we abandoned the belief that God made us the world's saviors, we find ourselves in a world that is in constant need of aid. And we go about giving that aid in the form of money, food, infrastructure, and pat ourselves on the backs for being humanitarians. Doesn't that sound like a self-fulfilling prophecy to you?

Chemotherapy causes cancer—in some cases just not quite as quickly as it cures the existing cancer.

Is it somehow possible that we ourselves created the conditions for this famine-plagued, impoverished world to exist that is in perpetual need of our care?

Neither our educators nor our history books ask the question, "How?" And they do not offer to explain.

Poverty is simply a fact of life. How is that any different from saying, "God made it that way?"

We feel guilty if we do not do the humanitarian thing and give aid. How is that different than saying, "God made us the saviors of the world?"

◇

POVERTY IS THE politically correct term for oppression.

There is no poverty. There is only oppression.

Poverty is an invention of civilization, a side-effect of wealth creation, of a disparity between the haves and the have-nots, Capitalism's collateral damage.

Sending food and money to the Third World is akin to treating a cancer patient with chemotherapy. (Chemotherapy causes cancer—in some cases just not quite as quickly as it cures the existing cancer.)

Daniel Quinn, a brilliant sociologist with a controversial theory, calls this *the population paradox*: that increased food production will always lead to increased population.

The problem today, at its core, is that we are importing food to areas of the world that cannot support the number their populations have swelled to. And why have they swelled to such numbers? Because every year we import more food than the last year—thereby ensuring in perpetuity that we will always have a self-fulfilling destiny to fulfill, even after we no longer believe it's our destiny.

Poverty is the antithesis of wealth.
One cannot exist without the other.

But why do we import more food each year? How did it come to be that the Third World *needs* to be on life-support?

<>

THERE ARE TWO lies we must first expose before we can begin to answer that question.

The first lie is that Third World countries have always and forever been poor and that it's only through the miracle of Western technology and the unprecedented wealth the First World has generated that people living in these areas don't have to endure even worse lives!

In other words, they should be grateful to us for doing everything we can to help them because they are unable to help themselves.

But that's simply not true. Poverty is the antithesis of wealth. One cannot exist without the other.

154   A PEOPLE'S HISTORY OF CAPITALISM

The economically anorexic populations among us, which we call *the poorest*, have become, in a world of 7 billion humans, unable to support themselves only because the most economically opulent hoard all the wealth.

The second lie is that we started delivering food to these areas to support poor populations out of a humanitarian sense of mercy for suffering people. Without that aid they would suffer even more!

The truth is, we send aid not out of a humanitarian sense of mercy, but out of a sense of guilt!

The truth is, oppression creates all the suffering in the world.

Before the Age of Imperialism, there was no Third World, no regions teaming with unsustainably large populations.

Now we're getting at the root of it.

Economic Imperialism caused poverty.

Ok....but how?

Let Their Be Poverty

BRING water to the desert, and the sands tend to bloom like the Garden of Eden. But the same is not true of bringing Capitalism to the rest of the world.

Yet that's exactly what Imperialists believed would happen. And so, from their Capitalist strongholds of Europe and America, in the 16th and 17th centuries, they set sail for Africa, South America and the Orient, confident that Civilization (by which they meant Western Civilization) would sprout up everywhere.

This Age of Imperialism would reach a fever-pitch from 1850-1914 before collapsing under its own weight.

Imperialists were more than a bit surprised that the natives' first reaction wasn't to kneel down at the feet of materialism, Capitalism and civilization.

From the beginning, Capitalist missionaries encountered peaceful, thriving agrarian and hunter-gatherer societies all over the world that were doing just fine on their own, thank you very much.

"No, no, no, you aren't civilized!" the Capitalist missionaries proclaimed. "Look here! What are you doing sitting around all day? You hunt and gather and then you take a nap? You lazy fools!"

On the West Coast of Africa, European colonizers transformed the land into gold and diamond mines and the people into slave laborers.

"Here's the deal," the Imperialists proclaimed, "Instead of being lazy your entire lives, we'll teach you what you obviously don't know: how to mine this land, which will bring your society extraordinary wealth! You will have metal armor like ours and own ruby rings like the ones we wear and your women will hang diamonds from their necks, and you will no longer live in huts, but palaces! Embrace Capitalism and you'll live like kings!"

Not that the natives ever really had much of a choice in the matter. "But why is this a good thing?" they asked. "Why is wealth and a life of hard work better than the lives of leisure we have as hunter-gatherers right now? We're well fed; we have each other, and we're happy."

The Imperialists were more than a bit surprised—and resentful—that the natives' first reaction wasn't to kneel down at the feet of materialism, Capitalism and civilization. But no matter, if the lavish decadence and temptations of materialist wealth wouldn't turn the natives, the Imperialist guns certainly would.

Poverty is an invention of civilization.
The Third World is an invention of Imperialism.

And so the peaceful lifestyles native societies had enjoyed for thousands of years were transformed overnight into daily drudgery, slavery and lives of backbreaking labor.

"Don't worry! All this hard work will be well worth it! We'll all be rich men!" said the Imperialists basking in the sun to the natives slaving in the mines.

Turned out, of course, that the Imperialists carted all the gold and diamonds back to Europe on their wooden ships and they alone became rich men.

In exchange for this, the Imperialists shipped European foodstuffs over to feed the natives, since they no longer had their own land or their own time.

And so it was that for the first time in history, the First World shipped food into the Third World. It had to. Because by now, all the ancestral hunting grounds had been carved into mines, and all the farming communities changed into slave camps.

◇

FROM THE GET-GO, there were a few problems with the food

that arrived from Europe, just as there have been problems with the whole arrangement ever since.

On the long trips from Europe to Africa, most of the food became infested with maggots. The rations that did survive the trip were not adapted to the new climate and, without proper storage, soon went rancid.

But where there's a will there's a way, and Imperialists certainly had the willpower. Without food, their new-found laborers would starve and couldn't work in the mines. With food, an ever-growing population of slave labor could be exploited.

Overcrowded cities popped up around the mines where peaceful villages had once stood.

> World hunger is the legacy of Capitalists'
> insatiable appetite for greed.

Imperialists invaded all the neighboring communities, always needing bigger mines and more slave laborers to work them.

The squalor and lack of sanitation in the new cities of this developing Third World were unmatched by anything in Europe or the young America.

◇

THINGS WENT ON much the same all over African, the Eastern colonies and Pacific Islands for a few centuries.

Then, two things happened:

1) The diamond mines, gold mines and all the rest had been largely excavated. There was no longer enough profits to be made to support colonialism.

2) Civilization of the Western variety didn't really take root in the colonies the way the Imperialists had predicted. Few colonies ever became "steady-state" societies. Without the artificial life support of European food subsidies, most conquered lands could never hope to support the populations that had grown up there.

So European and American colonizers woke up one morning, kind of scratched their heads and said, "Hmmm, well that didn't work."

And so, they picked up their things and sailed home.

They left as rich men, and left the colonies in squalor and poverty, the like of which the known world has never known. It has since been known as the Third World.

A century later, the United States has largely assumed the role of maintaining the food subsidies to the Third World, the need for which is the legacy of Imperialism.

Smallpox and poverty are only two of the diseases transmitted by Western Civilization. The others are greed and poverty.

We continue these programs out of a vague sense of guilt—even though most of us don't really remember and aren't taught what we're supposed to feel guilty about.

We do it also to focus people's attention on solving a problem (world hunger), instead of dwelling on the cause of poverty.

Too many of us donate pennies, never asking, "When and how did this situation begin? What went wrong?" World hunger is the legacy of Capitalists' insatiable appetite for greed.

◇

IMPERIALIST CAPITALIST MISSIONARIES bring the same two things to every people they conquer: outbreaks of smallpox and an infestation of poverty. Those are the two forgotten diseases Western Civilization infects the world with.

The Age of Imperialism didn't work, could never have worked, because it was founded on two faulty premises:

1) Affluent civilizations are based on the accumulation of wealth, not agriculture, labor, or the pursuit of happiness.

2) Once natives saw how well the West lived, they would instantaneously drop what they'd been doing for the past 10,000 years and join in the madness.

THE GUILT PARADOX

I APPRECIATE ice cubes on a hot day, hot water in the dead of winter, running water and flushing toilets. These were three of the things I missed most during the eight months I lived in Madagascar.

Living in the so-called "Third World" really puts things in a global perspective. It shows how sharp is the blade of the double-edged sword of progress.

> They are poor because you are not. They are poor
> because the life you live, the work you do, the
> crap you buy, enables the world that
> oppresses them to go round.

There are a few other luxuries I would have no idea how to go about living without because I've never had to.

Those include a furnace on a cold night, a soft mattress, an abundance of my favorite foods, always and forever, food without shortage.

We lump these together into the category of "a few of our favorite things." *Creature comforts* are the things technology has *blessed* us with.

Yet all the other creatures on the planet are perfectly comfortable without them. So I'd call these human comforts, but aborigines who have never known them don't miss them.

So they are actually the trappings of civilization.

Why trappings? Because we who have lived with them our entire lives don't know how to live without them. We imagine that survival without them could be nothing short of miserable.

We are told to appreciate them. We're made to feel guilty if we don't.

"Think of the poor starving children in Africa!" we're told when we don't finish all our vegetables.

Yes, think of the poor starving children in Africa. They are starving because we don't know how to live without all our favorite foods at our beck and call or ice or plumbing or a furnace.

They are poor because you are not. They are poor because the life you live, the work you do, the crap you buy, enables the world that oppresses them to go round.

Their lives are the collateral damage of ours.

And we're told to feel guilty, ashamed, if we don't appreciate what we have because people in the Third World don't have any of these things that make our lives bearable, livable.

It's a self-reinforcing delusion.

We are trapped. We will never know the simple pleasure of living simply.

Luxury becomes necessity. Things enslave us. We finance deficit lives. Debt is all our luxuries have ever bought us.

It's been quite a long while since I ascribed to the notion that the "Upper Class Dream" a.k.a. the American Dream—a huge house and a fertilized lawn, 2.5 children and 2.5 cars, washer, dryer, oven, gadgets, chemicals, cleaning agents—brings happiness.

It's a recipe for unhappiness. Addiction. Luxury becomes necessity. Things enslave us. We finance deficit lives. Debt is all our luxuries have ever bought us.

Yet even adopting that mindset, I'm still apt to feel the pangs of guilt. It was so ingrained I didn't recognize it was a vestige, a symptom, of the very mindset I had so long ago rejected.

I felt guilty that the poor starving children in Africa were poor starving children in Africa.

There are slums and ghettos in the poorest countries and in the world's most overpopulated cities beyond the wildest nightmares of upper class minds. These people live in unimaginable poverty.

What if you were born there? What if you were born in that situation?

I honestly don't know. None of us can. I'm sure it's horrible. Literally, unimaginably, horrible.

According to National Geographic, on a global scale, a salary of $18,000/year is all it takes to be considered Upper Class. Yet only a single-digit percentage of the world's population makes that in a year.

That same figure places Americans below the poverty line.

It's an unimaginably different world everywhere else.

Do we feel guilty about that?

Do we feel guilty about where we were born? How we live?

◇

SOME OF US, no doubt, could use a little empathy, a sense of guilt. But those of us who should are the ones who don't.

A Wall Street Billionaire's salary is a king's ransom to you.

But your annual salary is a king's ransom to a child in Africa.

Is there a single Wall Street Billionaire who feels guilty?

There are two kinds of peoples who live without running water and all the rest: The poorest of our civilization, and those peoples whose way of life has not been corrupted by civilization.

If you are not making your fortune by stepping on the backs of others, it is not you who should feel guilty.

You are not the exploiter of humanity. It is not you who has caused this.

Do not make the billionaires' lack of guilt your responsibility.

Nor let the apathy of the billionaires spill over to you.

But know that it is not your fault.

You could not have chosen the country or economic circumstance you were born into any more than the poorest child in Africa could have.

There needs to be a call to action. But it cannot be fueled by guilt.

◇

I DON'T KNOW why I was born where I was, when I was, who I was.

I have the means and ability to make the most of myself. The same cannot be said for children born in the slums of Africa.

I don't know why.

But it's a lie that I should feel guilty about it.

I appreciate ice cubes on a hot day, hot water in the dead of winter, running water and flushing toilets.

But having them makes us unable to appreciate a life without them. We are their slaves.

◇

AND THERE ARE more lies still.

Forget for a moment the victims of our civilization, the squalor and abject poverty of the Third World.

There are two kinds of peoples who live without running water and all the rest: The poorest of our civilization, and those people whose way of life has not been corrupted by civilization.

There are human lives that have never been impacted at all, neither positively nor negatively by our so-called civilization.

They live as they have for thousands of generations. Naturally.

Without running water. Without a surplus of food or a lack. Without any creature comforts whatsoever, or human suffering.

We're told these people should be *civilized* by us—that it's every human's God-given right to have access to plumbing, running water, indoor heating and air conditioning. If only everyone could live the way the Upper Class does. If only everyone could live the way America does.

In some cases, these aborigines themselves are corrupted by this lie. Yet their lives, simple, uncomplicated, with plenty of time for reflection and life in the dream-world, hold real meaning.

We live our lives in the quotidian (real) world and we think it's the only one we have to live in.

We have lost the knowledge of the spiritual worlds of our ancestors. When asked what we dream about, many of us would answer by reciting a list of material luxuries by rote. That's because we've lost touch with the true meaning of a *dream world*. We think it's where we go when we sleep. Or a child's world of make-believe.

The "real world" grown-ups live in is the world of make believe materialism. Filled by illusion and empty dreams.

But listen to children share their world that we dismiss as "make believe." It's much the same as the way aborigines describe the world they live their entire lives in.

Not just the children. All aborigines.

We feel guilty for them because they do not have access to our material, materialistic world.

But it turns out that the Dream World may actually be the Real World and the quotidian world grown-ups live in is the world of make believe materialism. Filled with illusion and empty dreams.

Some fascinating research has been done on this. Read Joseph Chilton Piere's *A Crack in the Cosmic Egg* for more.

Every product we buy, every trip to the mall, every molecule of high fructose corn syrup we eat poisons our bodies and minds and takes us another step away from the real world.

A PEOPLE'S HISTORY OF CAPITALISM

ALTHOUGH IT'S BEEN quite sometime since I've equated the American Dream with Ultimate Happiness, it took me a long time to realize that aborigines, untouched by our civilization, feel sorry for us as much as we do for them.

I know I can do nothing about my circumstances. I can neither change the fact I was born in America with a wealth of material opportunity, nor the fact that I cannot possibly learn to live in the dead of winter without a furnace.

My only solace is the hope that the Captains of Industry may, in their next lives, be reincarnated as the ghetto-dwelling victims of the civilization they have thrust upon the rest of us.

And that all the victims of civilization may be reincarnated into a the real world, which is not corrupted with greed, avarice and materialism.

Future Roulette

THERE is an imperfect scenario of the future we have to consider. One in which our civilization does not collapse as the 11th hour ticks into midnight. One in which our civilization does not re-make itself by overturning the Capitalist paradigm once and for all.

This is perhaps the most hopeful and the most frightening vision of the world your grandchildren will inherit.

If individuals fail to imagine a new world for themselves, if a black swan never materializes, corporations may remain in control for a long time to come.

If we can stave off global warming for longer than it takes us to actually deplete the world's resources of easy oil, there may be another Brave New World.

I believe the oil tycoons and Capitalists know they've plotted a collision course for civilization.

Phillip-Morris knew cigarettes caused cancer better than the victims themsleves. Nevertheless, they testified before Congress that their product did not cause cancer at all.

I believe that oil companies realize the realities of global warming. They realize as much as any scientist, government, activist, or individual that we are headed for collapse.

In our millenia-old bid for immortality, we may finally achieve it, not by building pyramids or creating endowment funds, but our civilzation will be remembered forever. We will be forever imortalized as the civilization that destroyed the world.

I believe the oil tycoons and Capitalists know they've plotted a collision course for civilization. They may have bandaged the eyes of some of their political zombies and selling the Kool-Aid to the rest of us, but they're not stupid enough to drink it.

So even as Corporatist politicians and CEOs alike claim they wholeheartedly believe Global Warming is the biggest scam ever perpetrated on the American People, that it's a left-wing conspiracy and all the rest, they're all the while playing the same hand as Phillip-Morris.

Their biggest fear is not that global warming exists but that the rest of us might do something about it before the proverbial 11th hour.

They want to be the ones to decide when the jig is up. Not forced into an early retirement.

Corporate America may be selling Kool-Aid to the rest of us, but they're not stupid enough to drink it.

Oil companies may indeed have a plan, one involving practical mass production of alternative energy and electric cars. They may have already devised a marketing strategy and have a business plan in place for making piles and piles of paper profit off it all.

They have no intention of going down without a fight, no intention of sailing into the sunset or going quietly into the night.

They know the twilight of Big Oil is upon us ... and that we're in the 11th hour and 59th minute, but we still have a good 59 second left.

As good as Capitalists are at manufacturing short-term profits, they are even better at profiting from calamity.

Millions of dollars were made shorting airline stocks a day before 9/11. Even more colossal sums were raked in by the Too Big To Lose banks by plotting our financial collision course.

Both were instances of a long-term strategy brilliantly engineered to kick in when the short-term pyramid collapsed.

The success of the overall plan depends on letting tragedy strike. Averting disaster would mean missing out on a huge capitalization opportunity.

◇

IT'S THE SAME with oil. The tycoons will continue to suckle every last drop from the teats of Mother Earth until not a single ounce more can be siphoned.

Then, only then, after the last precious drops sell at the pump for $100/gallon, and the last dollar is made, suddenly, the oil tycoons themselves swoop in, save us from the brink of collapse to the sound of wild applause.

They won't do that until the 59th second of the 59th minute of the 11th hour.

Corporations are playing a most dangerous game with our future. They may already have secret solar panels, but they don't have a crystal ball.

You have to manufacture a crisis to be a hero.

150 years from now, do the history books read, "And alas it was BP who saved the world from the jaws of death, the very brink of collapse as, like a Phoenix from the ashes, they finally resurrected their Global Solar Panels, which has been buried all along beneath the sands of the world's largest deserts. The surface area of the solar panels was larger than anything anyone had ever imagined, and provided enough energy to supply the world's needs for 300 years."

It is the most hopeful and frightening future I can possibly imagine. That it will be the Corporations who save us from themselves; strengthening their stranglehold, convincing all of us we owe all of them our lives.

But this is a most dangerous game of Russian Roulette they are playing with our future. They may already have secret solar panels, but they don't have a crystal ball.

A PEOPLE'S HISTORY OF CAPITALISM

I wonder, knowing that the end of oil and Global Warming are converging upon us, are the oil companies frightened by how quickly and violently the environment is fighting back already?

When the CEO of the Big Planetary Oil Exploitative hears of Hurricanes and Flooding and melting Ice Caps, does he recline upon his throne like the Emperor of the Dark Side and assert, "Everything is proceeding as I have foreseen it."

Or does he think to himself, "Oh, shit. There goes the planet."

Your Final
Wake-up Call

HUMANITY, led by the Capitalist Class, wakes up to find itself goose-stepping in the parade of progress, winding down a yellow brick road which leads to a bright light at the end of the struggle.

The light is green, but blinding. We can't see what's ahead, so we're left to imagine what it is we're heading towards. The people in the parade, seeing the green glow, envision a gleaming Emerald City with liberty and justice for all. We call the promised land Utopia.

In the utopia imagined by a Capitalist, everyone's rich and lives like kings. At least, everyone who's allowed to pass through the gates. But you have to be rich to get in.

But while we're day-dreaming of equality, the Capitalists leading the parade see a city of green paper money, a "Capital" City. They call the promised land Wall Street.

In the utopia imagined by a Capitalist, everyone's rich and lives like kings. At least, everyone who's allowed to pass through the gates. But you have to be rich to get in.

And that is not the vision of utopia that the majority of humanity for the majority of history has ever dreamed of.

◇

AS OUR PARADE moves closer to the city, evangelical economists preach from podiums, converting as many non-believers as they can, spreading the good word, trying to get everyone to willingly pay to pass through the pearly gates into the Kingdom of Capital.

Economists preach that the Kingdom of Capital will soon be upon us. And when it does, disbelievers will all burn in poverty. So pay to repent now, before it's too late.

So, what evidence do they point to that their Kingdom Come, their Will be Done, in America as it is in Africa?

They point to the extraordinary wealth created by the stock market, the most efficient vehicle of money-making known to man.

They point to economic success stories in the Second World, countries like Brazil, Russia, India, and China. Thanks to the unprecedented success of Capitalism, so much money has been created that the Second World now has emerging economies and wealthy cities and successful Capitalists living among them and functional banking systems and democratic governments.

A Capitalist's utopia is founded on greed, and is merely a mirage of self-deception.

They even look at the Third World countries like Madagascar, and point out that while just 50 years ago everyone was living in squalor, today there is an emerging Middle Class.

Economists admit to the extremely inequitable wealth distribution in the world, but point out that if you look at the larger picture, it's getting better and better all the time. People's lives all over the world are improving every generation, and it's all thanks to the free market, the stock market and economic success of the First World.

It's true that some citizens of these countries have drastically better living conditions than they did in the 1800s. There is an emerging Middle Class.

But that ignores the fact Capitalists created the impoverished living conditions in the first place. And it also pre-supposes once more that the Capitalist utopia is what we all should be striving for.

A Capitalist's utopia is founded on greed, and is merely a mirage of self-deception.

Capitalists may indeed believe that in their utopia, everyone would be rich and live as kings. But the truth is, in order for rich men to get rich and live as kings, they must do so by standing on the backs of the poor.

Without poverty, there can be no wealth.

Without wealth, there would be no poverty.

Painted as a heaven for all, indeed, the Capitalists' utopia could never be more than economic hell for most.

The guys at the tippy-top know this, believe they are rich because God favors them and believe that only they should be let through the pearly gates of economic heaven.

The *nouveau riche* make the best Capitalist missionaries;
There is no one more fanatical than a convert.

In the meantime, they send out missionaries to preach their religion of Money. These missionaries take the form of self-made-men, the *nouveau riche*, people who's grandparents were as poor as dirt. These people make the best missionaries because there is no one more fanatical than a convert.

These missionaries teach that the Kingdom of Capital can be ours, too. All we have to do is accept Capitalism, work hard, be slaves to debt, put in our time, and in utopia we will be greatly rewarded.

Alas, no, that is not the way of it. There must always be the rank and file followers goose stepping in the parade, factory and industrial laborers and slaves to debt. The economic elite could never have risen to the top without the masses supporting their climb. Their economic utopia could not exist were the rest of us not building it for them.

And believing the lie that we are building it for *everyone*, looking at our palace homes and tech-y-gadgets as proof, we, Middle America and the Middle Class of the Industrialized world,

A PEOPLE'S HISTORY OF CAPITALISM

are working against our own interest, and the interests of all humanity.

We are allowing it all to continue.

◇

IN THE UTOPIA I dream of, there is justice for Capitalism's Crimes Against Humanity.

There is Capitalist Punishment.

The end of the Roman Empire came when the aqueducts delivering water to the Capitol City, Rome, were destroyed by invading armies. This cut off the Empire's ability to support the huge number of people living there.

In a democracy ruled by Capitalism, we vote with dollars. Every dollar counts. So don't vote. This is one election you need to sit out to make your vote count.

So what is Capitalism's main artery? Its life blood? The one thing Capitalism would not be able to survive without?

We are.

First, we all must wake up and see that we are doing nothing more than goose stepping in a charade put on by Capitalists. And we must stop marching. We all must imagine a different way to live—one not consumed by material things. A simpler way. A way that will make us happier. Lead us to more meaningful, fulfilling lives, lived with each other, not with things.

But imagining a new way of life isn't enough. We have to start living it.

We must stop enabling the march of Capitalism. Without our participation, it does not continue. It cannot.

So how to we stop it? Where do we begin?

In a democracy ruled by Capitalism, our political vote may mean nothing. (But vote anyway.)

In a democracy ruled by Capitalism, we vote with our dollars.

Every dollar counts. We vote if we want Elmo or X-box for X-mas. The Capitalists need our vote. Every vote counts. So don't.

This is one election you need to sit out to make your vote count.

◇

TODAY, THE ROAD we've been on is no longer paved with gold bricks. It's now just a regular old street. And it's led us right into to a wall.

This is the outer wall fortifying the Capital City and it's blocking our path. For humanity to move forward and the human spirit to thrive once again, we must take action immediately.

We must tear down this wall.

"You see things; and you say, *Why?*
But I dream things that never were; and I say, *Why not?*"

—*George Bernard Shaw*

PART 5

Tear Down this Wall!

Humpty Dumpty Sat on Wall Street

THE 1% have crashed the world economy that gave rise to their class. Let's not play the part of the victim.

Destiny has a way of being self-fulfilling. Since the Capitalist Class believes that civilization is based on economics, they are going to be more shocked than the rest of us when the bottom falls out of that basket they've put all their golden eggs in.

(The egg-heads on the Stock Market News channels are more surprised than the rest of them.)

There's nothing so dangerous as someone who's convinced they're right, especially when they aren't.

While you, me, and the wall know that life and work and civilization itself can go on perfectly well (and better) in the absence of Wall Street Capitalism, the Capitalists are going to be massively disillusioned, and they're going to try their damndest to prove they're right anyway. They truly believe that civilization is based on the underpinnings of economics.

There's nothing so dangerous as someone who's convinced they're right, especially when they aren't. Both will go to any length to prove their convictions. Only the one who's wrong will never stop because no matter how far they go, might doesn't make right in the end.

So when the 1% truly brings down the world economy in their quest to prove their righteousness, they're going to bring all of civilization down with it, just to show they were right all along about economics being the foundation of civilization. Even if, in the final hour, they accept they were wrong (fat cat's chance), then just out of sheer resentment about being wrong they're going to do everything they can to bring civilization down along with them as we share their great fall.

That's what stubborn little kids do; and that's how Capitalists have been behaving for the past 500 years.

Crying, "Mine! Mine! Mine!" all the way to the bank.

But the 99% of us don't have to fall when Humpty Dumpy's Wall Street goes boom.

We can begin, right now, on an individual level, today, to start building a new way of life. To stop participating in the flawed system. Right now.

Imagine a new life, a new world, right now. Before the stroke of midnight.

We're already in the 11th hour. Let's get to work.

THE RULES OF CLASS WARFARE

THE Middle Class and Capitalism, two dichotomously op-
posed forces in today's world, both grew out of the same
time period in Western history.

Though their origins are linked, today they work at cross purposes. The only hope for the continued existence of a Middle Class
is an equitable distribution of wealth. And that's not the goal of
Capitalism.

The goal of Capitalism is a transfer of all the wealth to the top.

And today, the Capitalists are winning. If they ultimately do
win, where does that take us as a society?

It may collapse the Middle Class and they'll be no one left to buy
anything the Capitalists are pedaling. And thus collapses Capitalism, too.

Perhaps the only bad things happening in the world
are caused when we refuse to let go of old ideologies
after we've outgrown them. That's certainly true of Capitalism.

The transfer of wealth can only go on so long. At some point,
there's nothing left to transfer. It's like a poker game. One player
ultimately ends up with all the chips, and he's called the winner.

In the game of Capitalism, when the Capitalists end up with all
the chips, that brings us right back to where we started.

Perhaps back to a Feudal society, where there are only the oppressors and the oppressed. Compared to Feudalism, Capitalism
was quite an improvement.

Contemporary psychologist and philosopher William Meader
believes that the only bad things happening in the world are
caused when we refuse to let go of old ideologies after we've

outgrown them.

That's certainly true of Capitalism. If we can just learn to let it go, maybe we don't have to return to a feudal society. Maybe we can start over from the time just after feudalism collapsed. That's when the slate was wiped clean and we began again.

Though Capitalism needs a Middle Class to thrive, fortunately, as we'll see, a thriving Middle Class does not need Capitalism.

◇

THE MIDDLE CLASS has been struggling to survive ever since it emerged from the ashes of feudalism.

Under Capitalism, the Middle Class way of life has already reached its peak and is in decline.

> The transfer of real wealth is all but complete. The only thing left is the monopoly money they make on Wall Street.

Today, families who were firmly Middle Class a generation ago are now either falling back into poverty or managed to get off the elevator on the Upper Class floor.

Like we saw at the end of the Dark Ages, today, all the rules are changing.

Thanks to the stock market, among other factors, we are seeing a transfer of wealth to the very top at an unprecedented rate and scale—a scale analogous, I would say, to the population decline caused by the Black Plague.

The transfer of real wealth is all but complete. The only thing left is the monopoly money they make on Wall Street.

Capitalism never was and never will be a perpetual energy machine. The cycle of perpetual growth must end sooner or later.

All the rules are about to change one way or another.

SENTINELS OF THE PARADIGM

THE most important wars are not decided in a few short years. They extend down through the centuries, cultural revolutions waged by generation after generation. These are ideological revolutions, which, when successful, transition into societal evolution.

The wars to end feudalism, slavery, dictatorships and monarchies had innumerous bloody battlefields.

But it's not on the battlefield these wars were won. Victory was found by changing people's minds.

The only way to counter an idea is with another idea.

◇

THE WESTERN CULTURAL idea has been "might makes right." Too many revolutionaries have raised an army against the West by finding bigger guns, employing better armies. That's been the history of Western Civilization in a nutshell. When one culture enacts the "Three Beliefs" (which we first discussed at the outset) more effectively, the old Empire is overthrown and the new one emerges. The only problem with that scenario is that Western Culture wins either way. The West marches on.

When revolutionaries attack the sentinels of the existing paradigm with bigger guns, they are proponing the very idea they are fighting against: that "might makes right."

They might win the Battle of the Bigger Guns, but in the end, the old ideology lives to fight another day.

A Nation of Drunks

THERE were examples of seemingly spontaneous social reforms in the past. But those changes were not spontaneous at all.

The illusion of spontaneity comes when an idea seems to pop into almost everyone's mind virtually at the same time. What really happens is that when small, isolated groups of people think the same thought for long enough, suddenly, a critical mass of people is reached. At which point the idea begins spreading so quickly and exponentially that it seems to have generated spontaneously, like a wildfire in a dry forest.

The idea that we could prohibit alcohol in a nation of drunks? Almost as unthinkable as banning Capitalism in a nation of Capitalists.

The Prohibition movement offers an interesting example.

The movement against the consumption of alcohol had been around for nearly 100 years before an amendment to the constitution was proposed and ratified.

The truth is, America was a nation of violent drunks. The movement's original goal was to end the drunkenness, strictly regulate hard liquor, and even outlaw saloons, where all the drunkards got drunk. But never to outlaw alcohol altogether.

The activists took one step forward for every two steps back.

You can learn details from history books, but the central idea we're concerned with is this:

After 100 years of a small, powerful idea spreading slower than molasses, in the blink of an eye, after a century of getting nowhere, alcohol was suddenly illegal.

Not only saloons; not only hard liquor, but all alcohol. Everywhere.

Contemporary historians view the entire movement as some kind of mass hysteria that swept the country.

The idea that we could ban alcohol in a nation of drunks!? It was absurd. It was preposterous.

And then it happened.

> Banning Capitalism in a nation ruled by Capitalists?
> Maybe such a radical solution might just be enough
> to sober up all the Capitalist scofflaws drunk on greed.

All in all, prohibition was a terrible experiment. It created organized crime, the mafia, bootlegging, and a real mess.

It was repealed almost as quickly as it was enacted, as if we'd all awoken from some powerful trance.

But, guess what? The radical abolition of alcohol ended the era of the saloons. It resulted in heavy regulation of hard liquor. And it significantly impacted the problem of drunkenness.

But the idea that we could ban alcohol in a nation of drunks!?

Almost as unthinkable as banning Capitalism in a nation ruled by Capitalists. Yet maybe such a radical solution might just be enough to sober up all the Capitalist scofflaws drunk on greed.

◇

THE IDEA'S BEEN spreading for a little while now.

Maybe soon it will catch on like wildfire.

Let's a all do just a little. Attend one protest. Lift one finger. Tell one other person one thing you've learned.

GARDEN ROOTS MOVEMENT

GRASSROOTS implies that ugly green weed growing in your front lawn.

By "garden roots" I mean individuals convincing other individuals convincing other individuals.

Too many grassroots organizations that organize themselves around the shared mindset that big things happen from small beginnings betray their own fundamental premise too soon.

Grassroots organizations too often try to rally people to change the mindset of the existing hierarchy.

Society is changed by individuals, not by governments.

In other words, they take a bottom-up approach (by forming a grassroots movement) and then adopt a top-down method for bringing about change.

They spend enormous amounts of time and energy trying to convince the cogs of government to change policies, enact legislation., etc.

By their own admission, they understand that governments and hierarchies are well-fortified against outside thoughts and agendas, which, they will point out, is why they began their movement in the first place.

Yet somehow they think that with a large enough grassroots establishment, they can infiltrate the halls of government and make a difference. This often takes tremendous resources, time and money and usually meets with some small triumphs, which they then point to and say, "the journey of a thousand miles begins with the first step."

But fighting the existing establishment yields only small, Pyrrhic victories. So long as grassroots activists continue unbridled enthusiastic rejoicing after achieving each small morsels of success, the longer they will continue to do too little.

Traditional methods adopted by too many grassroots organizations shoot too high and miss. They aim for the big guns of government, trying to reach everyone by changing laws.

They might fight the good fight for a few years before changing a single piece of legislation.

But how many individual minds could they have reached in that same time?

Not enough, they say. And so they aim for the big guns of government who can reach *everyone* by changing the laws.

But by reaching out to individuals, not government, changing individual minds, we can change lives along the way.

We should not rely on governments to force people to do this thing or not do that thing.

Society is changed by individuals, not by governments.

Yet traditional methods adopted by too many grassroots organizations shoot to high and miss more often that not.

◇

HISTORY HAS SHOWN us time and again that when broad, sweeping change is thrust upon society, megalithic institutions are far too cumbersome to adapt quickly enough.

Only individuals survive.

The fall of the Roman Empire is a tragic example. Rome's politicians had become so corrupt, its armies over-extended, its treasuries depleted, its population too large and its grain stores too small, that there was no way the Empire could be reformed from within. The empire collapsed and the world was plunged into 1,000 years of darkness. The entire civilization had poured all its hopes into the Empire and when the empire collapsed, all of society came collapsing down with it.

Any grassroots organizations that may have existed at the time, fighting hopelessly to reform Rome from within, are lost to the annals of history. The ones so convinced that they could reform the Empire, right up to the last day, died with their heads in the sand.

They would have done well to direct their energies elsewhere. They would have done well to accept that the Empire was "too big to fail," and therefore, that it ultimately must.

Now, letting the Empire fail is not at all an endorsement of anarchy. It is the exact opposite.

I believe that as long as grassroots organizations continue beating down the walls of the establishment, so pigheaded in their naïveté of believing they can actually make a difference before it's too late, they are doomed to be buried in the avalanche when the walls come tumbling down.

We would do well to accept that anything
"too big to fail" ultimately must.

What can be done must come from a "garden roots" approach—one which shows people a different way to live.

We must accept that the establishment is doomed to fail, as well as all those who stand alongside it or within when the walls fall.

Members of garden roots movement will be individuals (perhaps small tribes) who have started to imagine and enact different lives for themselves, living apart from the establishment—not in opposition to it, just outside.

Neither outside the laws, nor inside them, simply separate.

These individual groups will survive any doomed society. If enough pockets of these individuals exist, they will have a ready-made framework for whatever is to come.

These garden root individuals will be the ones who ensure anarchy does not run amuck, that the world is not plunged into 1,000 years of darkness.

A PEOPLE'S HISTORY OF CAPITALISM

When the society that is "too big to fail" comes crashing down, they will already be living different lives and, by example, teach others how to do the same.

Think Outside the Dollar

GARDEN roots organization is not just a pun on the grassroots name.

It is an apt term because facing the current convergence of global crises, I believe the life we must imagine outside the existing paradigm, will be rooted in individuals growing their own food. These will not be individualists or survivalists living on a mountain somewhere. Now, more than ever, people will need to cooperate to survive and thrive.

Individual small groups of people that can learn to work together and develop locally-based communities that will thrive. We need to grow these communities now.

We all need to develop local communities, not economies.

Money cannot be the thing that makes them go round.

We can cut out corporate control from our lives by buying from local merchants or bartering with individuals.

There are towns, cities and regions in 36 of the 50 US states that use their own local currency in addition to the mighty dollar.

Don't hail to the hegemony of the all-powerful dollar.

◇

WE MUST RE-IMAGINE our cities.

All over America, the "downtowns" of most major cities have been converted into financial districts.

Once-quaint small towns and their downtowns have become nothing more than glorified shopping malls, mostly merchants selling things we don't need.

We need to re-create town squares where people come together to walk after dinner, to experience local bands on small venues. (Get rid of the electric amps, too.)

A PEOPLE'S HISTORY OF CAPITALISM

The other major move in re-imagining our cities is to once again make them places for people, not cars. You can hardly find a sidewalk anywhere that doesn't have a street with it.

With electric cars, we don't have to give up driving; nor do we have to give up walking or biking.

But I don't have any time for any of this, you say.
To which I say, make time not money.

Some cities are taking small steps in the pedestrian friendly movement. But we're walking when we need to be running.

Cars are not permitted on Mackinaw Island in the Upper Peninsula of Michigan. We need to have a car ban in more places.

It's essential for a re-imagined life.

◇

WHEN A SMOKER gives up cigarettes, one of the hardest things to do is to override the associations they have with smoking. Smokers have to re-learn that they can drink coffee without smoking, eat dinner without a cigarette.

Collectively, we need to remember that we can enjoy music without amps; communicate without e-mail or text or phone calls.

We need to remember how to dry our clothes without popping them into the dryer.

We can wash our cloths and dishes without machines, too.

We can enjoy a meal together without going to a restaurant.

But I don't have any time for any of this, you say.

To which I say, make time not money.

We can make a living without giving our lives to our jobs.

◇

SO MANY OF us have so much talent that we take up very fulfilling hobbies. I know many hobby enthusiasts who make a good living at their day job and use their hobby to escape. They then don't want to sell the things they make or lend the skills their hobby has developed for them to "making money." They use the hobby to escape that lifestyle.

How backwards is that?

If we can just give up our addiction to money, we might be able to remember how to provide for our own basic needs with a little help from our community and friends.

Often, hobbies nurture valuable skills that can be used to benefit others. This is how we can make a living without making money. If we all pursue our natural talents, we may just find we don't need jobs (or at least a 40-hour/week job) to support our lifestyle.

We all can and must find work that supports our lifestyle; the only lifestyle allowed by working all the time is a lifestyle of working all the time.

Just as we confuse money with wealth, we confuse our lifestyle with our career.

No this isn't something that will happen overnight.

Don't read this book and then quit your job tomorrow.

Don't join a commune.

Don't go live on a mountain somewhere.

Develop a community.

Imagine a new life.

◇

SOON, WHEN OIL prices triple, it may not be economical to drive to a job that pays the same as it always did. In other words, it may not make economic sense to work.

Consider these national averages, compiled from various sources and intended only as a rough estimate.

- **Day care:** $972/month
- **Lease on a second car:** $475/month.
- **Gas:** $175/month/vehicle (this is going to go up). Assume

it only doubles: $350/month/vehicle.
- **Car insurance**: $70/month
- **Taking the tollway to work**: $20/month.
- **Eating out:** $7,500/year more expensive than groceries.

That's an overall cost around $30,000 we spend on services and things that we could be doing ourselves if we had more time. Just about 40% of Americans make less than $35,000/year.

We are all "job creators." We employee machines to work for us. We outsource our lives to technology.

Those numbers just aren't adding up.

By "working for yourself"—you could have time to do work yourself—instead of having machines and technology work for you.

We are all "job creators." We employee machines to work for us. We outsource our lives to technology.

If we can just give up our addiction to money, we might be able to remember how to provide for our own basic needs with a little help from our community and friends.

We must learn how to rely on our local communities. Real people who we see everyday.

Blacklisted

EVER notice how you can criticize government all you want, but when you start criticizing Capitalism, you're quickly blacklisted as a Socialist?—Usually by people who don't know exactly what socialism is. They just kind of have this vague idea that it's kind of like communism and fascism.

It's not. Socialism is nothing like communism or fascism.

Being a libertarian (anti-government), that's ok. Governments of Kings and Dictators have been oppressing the People for millennia, so it's perfectly acceptable to channel your anger against them. But don't you dare start to criticize corporations! They are the ones here to protect you from the Big Bad Wolf of Government! Where would you be without Capitalism? The Soviet Union? Russia was an Evil Empire! Or so we're taught in school.

Ok, I'm not necessarily disagreeing with you, but can you tell me why exactly?

Because they were a Communist society!

What's a Communist society?

An Evil Empire!

Being a libertarian (anti-government), that's ok. But criticizing Capitalism and you're blacklisted as a Socialist

---

That doesn't explain anything.

We're taught that Socialism, Communism and Fascism are Bad Words in school, but we're never told what these things are.

Are they political systems, economic systems? Ideologies? Philosophies? What? And what about them is so bad?

And why are they all lumped together?

We're usually taught about these three things in the same

chapter of the History books, the one about World War II. So we kind of take away the impression that Socialism, Communism and Fascism are all kind of the same thing.

But the only thing they have in common is they all posed a threat (either real or imagined) to King Capitalism and were all promoted by revolutionaries in the early 1900s.

And that's all you need to know, kid. Capitalism prevailed. So you don't have to worry about any of those systems anymore.

And so all we have to go on is what we're told. (Or not told.) Just like all I had to go on was what CNBC was telling me before I woke up.

The only thing Socialism, Communism and Fascism
have in common is they all posed a threat
(either real or imagined) to King Capitalism.

And that shouldn't be good enough. It's not good enough.

I *am* going to question Capitalism. We all should. We've been a Capitalist society for so long that we just can't remember another way. Actually, we aren't *taught* the other ways.

But they exist. Go look.

I don't care if people who don't know what the word means call me a Socialist.

By the way, can you honestly say you know what the word Socialism means? I'm just curious.

Sorry, that's the topic of a whole other book. That opens a whole other can of worms.

I don't want this to turn into a political rant.

CAPITALIST PUNISHMENT

S○ we've seen that an economy based on financial services is itself the ultimate pyramid scheme. The stock market enables this more than anything else. The Stock Market is the ultimate Weapon of Mass Destruction in the Capitalists' Arsenal, generating the illusion of wealth that enables all the other things.

Most us, I believe, would call Wall Street an Evil Empire.

So I think Wall Street then, the Capital Capitol of the World, is the best place to start looking for what justice there can be for the exploits of pathological greed, waging an Oedpial Oil War that's devouring Mother Nature, and the all out economic *coup d'étas* of our entire civilization.

They've constructed a paper pyramid of stocks.
The punishment should fit the crime.
Capital Punishment for Capitalism
is tearing down Wall Street.

How can the builders of the Great Pyramids of Paper money be brought to justice? What Capitalist Punishment can future generations seeking justice possibly pass down?

The punishment should fit the crime.

The worst crime is the construction of the paper pyramid built by the Stock Market.

So the Capital Punishment for that system—the Death of Capitalism—would be tearing down Wall Street.

But how the heck do we do that?

TEAR DOWN THIS WALL STREET!

This isn't a physical wall like the one President Reagan wanted destroyed when he demanded, "Mr. Gorbachev, tear down this wall!"

No, you can't Tear Down This Wall Street with chisels and pick axes, or even with an army of bulldozers.

And even if you could, that surely would open the flood gate for the downfall of civilization as we know it. As things stand, our entire civilization is supported by Wall Street's paper pyramid. We can't just destroy the base and expect civilization not to collapse down upon us.

The stock market is an idea. It's infected every walk of life. Its foot soldiers have infiltrated the World Wide Web.

This is not a war we can wage against the physical New York Stock Exchange, the Chicago Board of Trade or the office buildings on Wall Street.

The stock market is so much more. It's an idea.

It's infected every walk of life. Its foot soldiers have infiltrated the World Wide Web. There are legions of Internet traders, making millions, producing nothing while sitting behind their "Strategy Desks" every day, working right from home.

Economic Civilization is a paper pyramid, and we are all playing the part of Atlas, standing inside, holding it up. We must set it down very gently.

It can't be torn down by an army.

We have to choose to exit, one by one.

◇

PRESIDENT REAGAN WOULD probably be rolling in his Republican grave to hear his words appropriated to refer to Wall Street rather than the Berlin Wall.

Later in that same speech, he quoted graffiti written on the wall itself:

"'This wall will fall. Beliefs become reality.' Yes, across Europe, this wall will fall. For it cannot withstand faith; it cannot withstand truth. The wall cannot withstand freedom."

AN UNEMPLOYED ARMY

WE are writing our own graffiti now on Wall Street. Official numbers claim the unemployment rate in America hovers around 10%. I think we all know that's fuzzy math, and the real number is closer to 25% or 30%.

Worldwide, the situation looks grim. The entire worldwide economy of the global Imperialist Economic structure teeters on the verge of collapse.

During the American Great Depression of the 1930s, unemployment peaked around 28%. It was just as bad in Europe, especially in Germany.

But all told, there were only 2 billion humans living on earth in the 1930s. Today there are 7 billion.

So use whichever unemployment numbers you want. Either way, there is a huge standing army waiting to be deployed.

There are 300 million people living in America today. If our unemployment rate today were the same as that of the 1930s, that would mean there are almost as many unemployed Americans as the entire population of Americans in the 1930.

◇

THAT'S A HUGE group of people who, at the moment, don't seem to have a place in the fabric of our economically hierarchical society. That society is driven by a workforce.

In that society, we are our jobs. If we have no job, we don't fit in.

Does that sound right to you?

People's lives and identities should not be determined by who they work for. People's worth should not only be valued by how much money they make.

Yet that's the society we've built over the past 500 years.

One brick at a time.

But now we've hit a wall.

Modern ideologies can progress no further.

Our society has backed its own people into a corner.

I said the call to Tear down this Wall Street can't be accomplished with bulldozers or an army—but rallying the troops is a damn good place to start.

◇

OUR ARMY ISN'T comprised of revolutionaries; this isn't a revolution. This has the underpinnings of social evolution.

The very existence of the Unemployed Class will threaten the very hierarchy which gave rise to it. Just as the Middle Class did to feudalism.

We have an Unemployed Army. And that's where it starts.

Young and old, employed or not, have joined them.

And they're occupying Wall Street right now.

Support our troops. Write your own graffiti on that wall.

◇

THE WALL WILL fall; the pyramid will crumble. All of us, individually and together, must right now, today, begin to build a new foundation before the collapse comes, so that we don't get buried in the rubble.

That doesn't mean going back to a noble savage lifestyle, living in caves, hunting and gathering, being an anarchist, a libertarian, or even returning to a pre-industrial lifestyle.

It only means conceiving of a non-hierarchical society that manifests an affluent way of life for everyone. One where technologies are pursued not by the color of money but by the potential they have for building a better life for everyone. One where science is pursued for science's sake.

Yeah, yeah, yeah, I know. Sounds like the nonsense of King

Arthur and the Round Table.

... where everyone is equal, even the King.

Or John Lennon's imaginings that got him assassinated.

...brotherhood of man...

Or worse yet the rantings of the revolutionaries of the early 20th century.

...each according to his ability. Each according to his need.

◇

UTOPIA, A PERFECT society. A civilization that actually works for everyone.

It's a dream. An age-old dream that's never died.

It's a dream that's certain to out-live Capitalism.

Hope is a much better, stronger base for civilization than economics.

I hope we can hold onto that dream to get us through. It could be a nightmare when Capitalism collapses under its own weight if we don't have something to take its place. Or at least something to hope for. Some motivation other than profit to help us achieve something far better.

The rules are about to change all over again.

With each successive rise and fall, civilization has taken one step closer to achieving utopia.

I hope.

"Don't be deceived when they tell you things are better now. Even if there's no poverty to be seen because the poverty's been hidden. Even if you ever got more wages and could afford to buy more of these new and useless goods which industries foist on you and even if it seems to you that you never had so much, that is only the slogan of those who still have much more than you. Don't be taken in when they paternally pat you on the shoulder and say that there's no inequality worth speaking of and no more reason to fight because if you believe them they will be completely in charge in their marble homes and granite banks from which they rob the people of the world under the pretence of bringing them culture. Watch out, for as soon as it pleases them they'll send you out to protect their gold in wars whose weapons, rapidly developed by servile scientists, will become more and more deadly until they can with a flick of the finger tear a million of you to pieces."

—Jean Paul Marat
18th Century French Visionary

"When people feel themselves powerless to change fundamental aspects of their world, they begin to make accommodations with "realities" that they actually detest."

—Michael Lerner
The Politics of Meaning

"If the American people ever allow private banks to control the issue of their money, first by inflation and then by deflation, the corporations that will grow up around them (around the banks), will deprive the people of their property until their children will wake up homeless on the continent their fathers conquered."

—Thomas Jefferson
America's 3rd President; Writer of the Declaration of Independence

APPENDIX

A Capitalist's History of the Western World

Great Moments in the
History of Capitalism
Part I: 1348-1900

The Origins of Capitalism

1348
The black death spreads across Europe, causing a population decline on an unprecedented scale. The old rules governing society are thrown out the window. Age of Feudalism ends ... and gives way to Capitalism.

c. 1350-1400
The world's first Merchant Middle Class arises from the ashes of the black death, making their living trading goods from the East.

c. 1350-1400
Successful Merchant Middle Class members transition into the first members of a brand new Capitalist Class. One definition of 'Middle Class' equates it with the original definition of a Capitalist: someone with so much capital that they could rival nobles.

1397
The origins of the modern, private banking industry emerge in Italy with the establishment of the Medici Bank by Giovanni Medici.

1407
The earliest known government run deposit bank, Banco di San Giorgio (Bank of St. George) is founded in Genoa, Italy.

1600
The First World Empire founded as a commercial venture is incorporated, The

British East India Company.

1606
The world's first Stock Market begins in Holland.

1636
The first Stock Market bubble, Tulip mania, inflates in Holland. Single tulip bulbs sell for more than 10 times the annual income of a skilled craftsman.

1637
The tulip bubble pops.

1679
John Locke , widely known as the Father of Liberalism (limited government and free trade), writes the *Two Treatises of Government*.

1735
The British East India Company becomes the first corporation in history to raise its own military. The idea of a Capitalist Corporate Empire is emerging. Previously, from Rome to Britain, the only Empire the world has known was State-controlled .

Capitalist Empires, known as Monopolies, have arrived.
Government Empires, known as Monarchies, are threatened.

1757
Victory for the British East India Company in The Battle of Plassey establishes the world's first Corporate Colony on the Indian Subcontinent.

The line between Capitalism and State continues to blur. The War of Corporations and State has begun. The prize of victory will be Empirical Control of the World.

1773
Maintaining an army (and corruption) has brought East India Company Empire close to bankruptcy. It begs the Crown for help. The world's first corporate bailout passes through Parliament.

1773
The Age of Economic Imperialism is firmly established. Parliament has gained two seats on the East India Company's board of directors as part of the terms of the bailout. A blending of Corporate interests and State interests has begun.

A PEOPLE'S HISTORY OF CAPITALISM

1775–1783

Free Trade and Monopolistic practices are more at issue than any beef the 13 American colonies have with the British Crown in the first major Economic World War. Victory for the revolutionaries creates the United States of America.

1792

The Buttonwood Agreement, signed by 24 of the most influential Capitalists in the United States, establishes the beginnings of Wall Street.

1890

The principle of Economic Imperialism (already in practice for at least 100 years) is articulated in print in Alfred Marshall's *Principles of Economics*.

This spreads the cancerous meme that economics is the very foundation upon which civilization stands. Economic interests are said to be at the heart of everything: government, laws, family, tastes, sociology, culture, religion, war, science, research, art, irrational behavior, rational behavior, politics, law and crime.

c. 1800-1900

The Industrial Revolution is a huge boon for Capitalism. Mass production and the construction of a global industrial infrastructure allows the Capitalist Class to accumulate more wealth than ever before.

Great Moments in the History of Capitalism
Part II: 1900 - 2000

The Axis of Corporate Evil and the Capitalist Takeover of the World

c. 1900-2000

The world's average per capita income increases more than 10-fold, while the world's population increase more than 6-fold.

Capitalists have more consumers to sell more crap to than ever before. Money begins growing on trees.

1902

The roots of the Fascist ideology (State controlled Capitalism) begin in Italy. Corporations, in their bid to oust government from power have decided, 'if you can't beat 'em, join em.'

1907

The first Wall Street panic. Eight hundred million dollars in securities are unloaded within a few months. Stock prices plummet and runs on banks become a daily occurrence. Powerful Capitalist Tycoon JP Morgan pressures the leading New York bankers to forestall a total financial collapse of the country by setting up a single banking trust, with most large banks across the U.S. contributing to its financing. Morgan's own group, as you might imagine, has controlling interest. The era of Too Big To Fail has begun.

1908

Henry Ford complements mass-production with mass-assembly. This drives down production costs of complex items considerably, and allows Ford to market his Model-T to the Middle Class.

Other Capitalists soon follow suit, and material goods start selling like wildfire to everyone, lower class, Middle Class and upper class alike.

1929

The Second Wall Street panic. Stock prices rise way beyond any relationship with the actual worth of their companies. In 1929, stock prices are 400% higher than they were in 1924. The insiders have made their fortunes and can no longer sustain the con, so on October 23, 1929, the bubble bursts.

1931-1940

In response to the Great Depression, the top tax rate on the top 1% of the wealthiest Americans skyrockets from 25% to 81% to help ensure they can never accumulate that much capital again and destroy the economy.

This is a major victory for People and Government over Financial Capitalist Control. The immense transfer of wealth to the top 1% is stalled, creating a Middle Class that will thrive for the next half century.

Corporations don't like it much, but benefit from the huge wealth and population increase among the masses. More Middle Class people means more crap they can sell. Corporations and State are enjoying an uneasy stalemate.

1967

The Financial Capitalists are getting restless. This stalemate has gone on long enough. They break with the rest of the Corporate Empire, eager to get back into the ring and engage government once again.

To do it, Finance Capitalists need a new weapon, and they find it in idea of disintermediation—"eliminating the middle man." They apply the concept to money for the first time. That means it's now possible to make money by making money instead of making money by making products. In this case, the product itself was the "middle man."

Derivatives markets and credit markets spread like wildfire across Wall Street. The bubble of all bubbles, the money bubble, begins to inflate.

1973 - 1979

The U.S. Oil crisis in 1973 and the Energy Crisis in 1979 sees another faction of Corporate interests consolidate power. The war of Corporation vs. State is now being fought against on two fronts against two major Corporate Powers. On the front lines stand the Finance Capitalists and Big Oil.

1980-1988
Disintermediation is a huge success. Finance Capitalists have created enough Monopoly Money to buy a pivotal presidency and they install Ronald Reagan.

Reagan obediently slashes taxes on America's wealthiest 1% from 70% to 28%, and wealth resumes its unprecedented transfer from the Middle Class to the Capitalist Class.

This begins to starve the American government of revenue and the national deficit skyrockets. Financial Corporations have earned another major victory over government in their Corporate Takeover of the World.

In addition to Big Oil and Finance Capitalists, other corporate armies arise, including Agri-business, Pharmaceuticals, Health Insurance and Corporate Media, among others.

1982-1988
Government de-regulation of Corporations begins under President Ronald Reagan, another major victory for all Corporations in their war against the State, though Finance Capitalists arguably capitalize the most.

Deregulation allows engineered financial bubbles to begin inflating exponentially, and on an unprecedented scale.

1980-1990
Financial Corporations fully penetrate the Middle Class market as the number of credit cards more than doubles, and deficit spending increases more than five-fold. The average household credit card balance rises from $518 to nearly $3,000.

This credit card has emerged as a weapon of mass destruction of the Middle Class. People are quickly becoming slaves to debt.

1987
The Third Wall Street Panic.
"Black Monday" occurs on October 19th. The Dow Jones falls an astounding 508 points, the largest one-day loss in the stock market's history. The insiders running the con game land on their feet and quickly misdirect the public's attention, laying the blame on computerized trading. Individual investors are

A PEOPLE'S HISTORY OF CAPITALISM

stranded when prices fall.

1990

The Gulf War begins. It is the First World Oil War. Big Oil has hoodwinked the governments of the Industrialized World to finance Corporate Armies with tax dollars. This eliminates the problem of military action cutting into shareholder profits.

In holding the reigns of the strongest Superpower's military, Big Oil asserts a major victory over Government and their Finance Capitalist rivals in control over the State and domination of a One World Empire.

Big Oil brilliantly implemented a strategy which effectively uses the State's own military to fight alongside the Corporatists.

1994

Free Trade policies rise to ascendency, a victory for all Capitalist corporate factions. Free trade places Capitalist Economic interests firmly above Economic Interests of the People and the State. This begins to cause serious deficits in tax revenue and governments slide deeper into debt.

Great Moments in the
History of Capitalism
Part III:2001 -2011

The United Corporations of America

2001
The Second World Oil War begins. People are hoodwinked into believing this is a political war in response to 9/11. For the most part, we completely ignore the corporations behind the curtain.

2005
The world flattens. Globalization becomes a politically correct term for Economic Imperialist expansion.

Early 2008
The third stock market panic begins as people start paying attention as the artificial "housing bubble" continues bursting. The bubble's been bursting since 2000; though hardly anyone has noticed; it started inflating in 1987; housing prices had quadrupled in the intervening 13 years.

Mid 2008
On the heels of the housing bubble bursting, it's revealed that Insiders had taken out insurance policies, ensuring they'd profit when it popped. It's revealed that Capitalists have found a strong ally in Insurance Companies, whom they have joined forces with against their mutual enemies, the State and the People.
The Financial Capitalists have been getting arrogant. They have switched from a fascist strategy of "if you can't beat 'em join 'em" to a libertarian strategy of "if you can't join 'em, beat 'em."

October 3, 2008
The Day that Rome Fell.

Financial Companies are going bust left and right on the heels of the global economic meltdown. (Don't worry, financial corporations aren't really in trouble; this is just a head-fake which turns world governments into shills in the con game).

Banks cry wolf, claiming that if they go bust, the world economy goes bust.

The "TARP" bailout package is ramrodded though the United States Congress, which would give billions of dollars to the Financial Capitalists. A first vote in the House roundly rejects the measure.

Finance Capitalists engineer a second vote for TARP, this time purchasing the votes they need.

The vote on October 3rd, 2008 is nothing less than an economic coup d'état of the United States Government.

This is viewed by future historians as the day the United States of America became the United Corporations of America. They equate this day to the assassination of Julius Caesar, when the Republic of Rome fell and the Roman Empire began.

Bailout measures have passed in Europe as well as billions of dollars are defrauded from the United States Treasury and the other world governments.

People and governments alike are now enslaved by debt. The people's last lines of defense against a Corporate Takeover teeter on the brink of collapse.

The CNBC anchor affectionately known as the money honey says, "What the heck just happened here? No one knows!"

November 2008

Finance Capitalists are patting themselves on the back for their major world victory in the battle of the TARP. Wall Street becomes the new Globalized Corporate Capitol; Pennsylvania Avenue in Washington D.C. is renamed "Sesame Street," because that's where the puppets live.

But not all Capitalist corporations are happy.

What remains of the splintered American manufacturing base doesn't like that the banks are hoarding all the power, and holding the Middle Class hostage.

The Middle Class, aren't buying enough crap anymore.

Corporate profits grow anemic, the stock market collapses to new lows and the price of oil triples.

2009

American Manufacturing Corporations that aren't in on the take file for bankruptcy.

Banks see these corporations as relics of a by-gone era. "You're still making products!?" they decry. "Geez, this is the 21st century! Money is the only real product, don't you know that?"

A factional group of Capitalists ban together to finance an army dubbed the Tea Party. It will fight against Financial Capitalists and what's left of the U.S. Government alike. A Capitalist Civil War is beginning.

2010

The Tea Party is mostly ineffective, but manages to install a few Corporate shills into the House and Senate.

The Corporations of America negotiate an uneasy truce with each other. The terms of the armistice carves up the last remnants of the United States political government between various corporate interests.

Wall Street becomes the First Emperor Augustus; Big Oil will maintain control over the military arm of government; a hybrid Agricultural/Chemical Industry hog-ties the FDA; and the Pharmaceutical Industry holds the AMA hostage.

Other minor skirmishes take place on the Corporate theatre, but in general, power has been consolidated in the United Corporations of America.

Even where they don't agree, Corporations from all walks of greed ban together in solidarity and maintain a media blackout.

2011

What?! Just as we've finally managed, after 500 years, to beat government into submission, now we have to worry about a popular uprising!?

The Occupy Wall Street movement begins a People's Revolution to Tear Down

Wall Street.

The CNBC anchor affectionately known as the money honey asks, "What the heck are we protesting here? No one knows!"

What happens next is anyone's guess. What I'd like to think happens....

20??

The CNBC anchor affectionately known as the money honey finally wakes up when the money bubble bursts. A mummified zombie hoard that includes politicians, news anchors, registered Republicans and others begins to wander the streets aimlessly as their tattered bandages of paper money unravel. The exposed zombie creatures don't have a clue what to do now.

But the rest of us do. Wall Street collapses, and humanity finally moves forward.

Corporate Think

◇

DOUBLE THINK : An idea created by George Orwell in *1984. (the novel)*. Meaning: when the brainwashed masses think twice about a blatant lie, reinforced so often that it becomes the believed truth.

◇

CORPORATE THINK : An idea created by Capitalists in 1996. *(the year Fox News was founded)*. Also known as Capitalist Think. Meaning: when the brainwashed masses *don't* think about a blatant lie, because they've never been told any different.

Here, then, is a list of some of the most common examples of Corporate Think.

◇

CORPORATETHINK:
- The success of a society should be measured by its affluence.

Origin:
- The Upper Class and Capitalist Classes.

Truth:
- The success of a society should be measured by how well it cares for its least privileged and how large a disparity exists between rich and poor.

◇

- The stock market measures the affluence of society and the success of a civilization. A rising stock market means a strong economy.

Origin:
- Capitalist rule in America is a staunch advocate of this idea.

Truth:
- A Stock Market measures the wealth of the richest people of a society.
- Stock prices rise only when rich people have excessive, disposable, investment income. This always creates an artificial bubble economy.
- A stock market crash means the richest 1% are unhappy. The economy is not transferring enough wealth to them. Like spoiled brats, they then set out to sabotage the economy for the rest of us. Mine! Mine! Mine! If I can't have it all, no one can!

◇

- Japan's economy has experienced no growth for 20 years as evidenced by their flat stock market. Their economy is in permanent recession.

Origin:
- Capitalist rule in America is a staunch advocate of this idea.

Truth:
- The gap between rich and poor in Japan has been narrowing.
- The Middle Class is prospering.

- Corporations and the richest 1% are job creators. High taxes prevent them from doing their job of being job creators.

Origin:
- Corporations and the richest 1% rule America.

Truth:
- Corporations don't create jobs. Demand creates jobs. The richest 1% really don't care about making jobs, just making money. Making jobs cuts into making money.
- Lower taxes on the wealthy puts more money into the deepest pockets and makes the stock market go up, up and away.

- Fascism, Communism, Nazism and Socialism are synonymous.

Origin:
- We were fighting against all four in World War II, so they must be the same thing.

Truth:
- Communism is a far, far left ideology. It's a perversion of socialism. We were fighting against it for Capitalist reasons.
- Socialism is a left wing ideology. It holds that Government should be responsible for ensuring that there is an equitable distribution of wealth. It does not take away the profit motive like Communism, but does makes excessive profits subject to extremely high levels of taxation. Capitalists

A PEOPLE'S HISTORY OF CAPITALISM

imagine it threatens Capitalism. Rather, by strengtheing the Middle Class, it supports Capitalism. Socialism can be thought of as a "trickle-*up* system."

- Nazism is radical white supremacy. We were fighting against Nazism for humanitarian reasons.

- Fascism is a far-far right political ideology. It is a merger of State and Corporate interests: we were fighting against it for Socialist reasons. It started as a merger of left and right ideologies: let's cut the size of government (the right) not by cutting programs, but by making it more efficient (left.) But Fascism degenerated into: the best way to create an efficient government is to run it like a business, and make the profit motive key. There isn't any distinction between Corporate and State interests (far-far right.)

◇

CORPORATETHINK:

- Socialism is evil. Socialism is Communism. Socialism takes away the profit motive and handcuffs corporations so that they cannot make money at all. All economies and all people under socialist regimes suffer as a result. There are no Socialist countries today. Socialism undermines democracy and Capitalism. Socialist regimes exercise absolute control over the countries they rule.

Origin:

- A strong socialist movement severely threatened Capitalist control of the United States from 1876-1920. This is not taught in history books because of the severe perceived threat it posed and the fear of it ever happening again. Instead, Socialism is implied to be directly related to Nazism and Communism.

Truth:

- The Socialist Labor Party (founded in 1876) and the Socialist Party of America (formed in 1901) worked on behalf of distraught workers and all oppressed people.
- The Socialist Party managed to successfully run hundreds of candidates for various political offices around the nation for several decades.
- Middle class and people in general thrive under socialism.
- Socialism does not undermine Capitalism. It merely keeps it from getting out of control and exploiting and subjugating people.
- Socialism, Democracy, and Capitalism can co-exist peacefully. They do in Europe. Most European countries today are socialist-leaning.
- Socialism is not a form of government or economics, but a point of view or ideology, like "Republican" and "Democrat."
- Socialism is not absolute. It is a sliding scale. Countries can have socialist programs, like Welfare, Medicare and Universal Health Care, but not be fully socialist.

A PEOPLE'S HISTORY OF CAPITALISM

Capitalist Think

◇

CorporateThink as it applies specifically to the role of Capitalism and how it gives us a Great Society.

Origin:
- All CapitalistThink thoughts share the same origin:
- Capitalism has been on the rise in the Western World for the last 500 years. Capitalists rule America today.

Here, then, is a list of some of the most common examples of CapitalistThink.

◇

CAPITALIST THINK:
- Capitalism creates wealth.
- Capitalism is the only means by which society grows in affluence. Capitalism has created our civilization.
- Capitalism gives tycoons the motivation necessary to advance civilization.

Truth:
- Capitalism does not create wealth; Capitalists hoard wealth.
- Labor creates wealth; Capitalism exploits labor.
- Capitalism is the way in which the Capitalist Class, not civilization, grows in affluence.
- Capitalism gives tycoons leave to be greedy.
- Profit is not a way to motivate, it is a way to exploit.
- Capitalists do not build civilization, they make slaves build it for them.

- Everyone in America is a Capitalist because we live in a Capitalist society.

Truth:
- A Capitalist is nothing more than a Class. The Capitalist Class is the aristocracy in a Capitalist Society.
- A Capital Class can arise in any society, including under socialism, dictatorships, monarchies, etc. Anywhere. But in those other societies, Capitalists are not the aristocracy because money is not the root of all power. That's only true under Capitalist regimes.
- The profit motive suppresses the rise of civilization. It only supports the rise in certain key areas, the areas that promise to make the most money.

- All great advancements happen because there was profit to be made. Without the promise of profit, we wouldn't live in the technologically advanced civilization of today.

Truth:
- Capitalism did not give us the technologically advanced civilization we have today. Science and Industry did.
- The Capitalist exploitation of science gave us a civilization filled with gadgets.
- The Capitalist's idea of 'a practical application,' as always, is to sell crap to make money.
- The main motivation for the advancement of civilization has always been war and Empire building. That's what gave us the Iron Age; that's what gave us the Space Race.

Profit had nothing to do with going into space. The Cold War brought us there.

◇

- The Corporate Takeover of the World is motivated purely by profit. Corporate control is more efficient than government control.

Truth:

- It's not motivated purely by profit. It's motivated primarily by a desire for control. The war against governments is waged by corporations seeking ultimate power.
- Corporations use capital and profit to gain control; Governments use their military and guns; Capitalism is merely a weapon of mass destruction in a war for conquest.

◇

- Capitalism is good for the betterment of all people and civilization itself.

Truth:

- Capitalism stunts the advancement of civilization because it places the need for profit above all things, including progress, pursuing *only* technologies that promise profit.
- There are many other motives that can build a civilization, many more motivational that the profit motive.
- In addition to conquest, other motivations include: a better life for all, the quest for an equitable civilization, and science for sciences' sake.
- All of these other motivations are suppressed when Capitalists control all the wealth of a society and decide exactly how it should be allocated.

Income Distribution in America

2010

								$1,600,000
$65,000	$80,000	$91,202	$100,000	$118,200	$166,200	$200,000	$250,000	
34.72%	25.60%	20.00%	17.80%	10.00%	5.00%	2.67%	1.50%	0.12%
Top third	Top quarter	Top quintile	Top 15%	Top 10%	Top 5%	Top 3%	Top 1.5%	Top 0.1%[10]

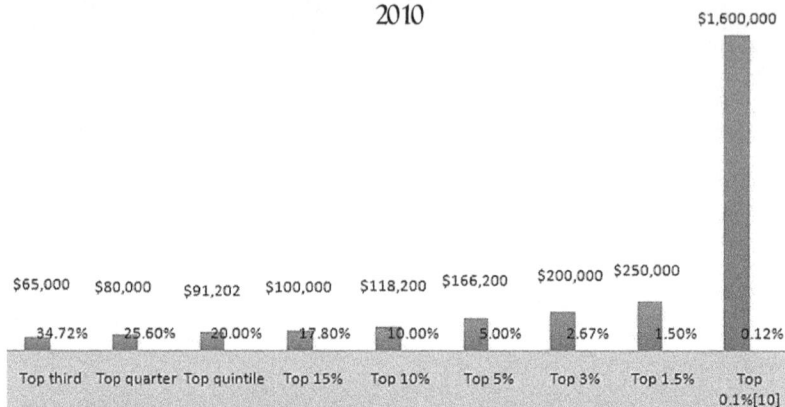

Income Distribution in the World*

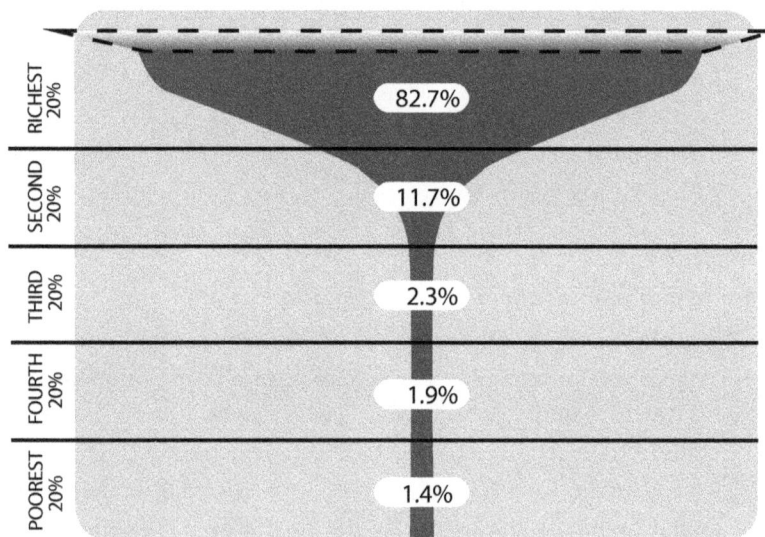

RICHEST 20%	82.7%
SECOND 20%	11.7%
THIRD 20%	2.3%
FOURTH 20%	1.9%
POOREST 20%	1.4%

Source: UN Development Program, 1992

* This is unfortunately old data, but this rendering, published by the UN, beautifully illustrates exactly how the "trickle-down" system doesn't work. A funnel is created, and the bottom gets, literally, a trickle. The inequality of wealth has gotten far worse over the past 20 years., but the actual numbers are largely immaterial (no pun intended) for our purposes. It's the concept illustrated here that I want to demonstrate, not to shock you with statistics. The dotted line at the top is a projection of how this graph would look if it were to show that the top 1% in the top 20% controls upwards of 95% of the wealth in their category.

A PEOPLE'S HISTORY OF CAPITALISM

Historical American Top Tax Rates

31-Jan-11

Historical Highest Marginal Income Tax Rates

Year	Top Marginal Rate	Year	Top Marginal Rate	Year	Top Marginal Rate
1913	7.0%	1946	86.45%	1979	70.00%
1914	7.0%	1947	86.45%	1980	70.00%
1915	7.0%	1948	82.13%	1981	69.13%
1916	15.0%	1949	82.13%	1982	50.00%
1917	67.0%	1950	91.00%	1983	50.00%
1918	77.0%	1951	91.00%	1984	50.00%
1919	73.0%	1952	92.00%	1985	50.00%
1920	73.0%	1953	92.00%	1986	50.00%
1921	73.0%	1954	91.00%	1987	38.50%
1922	56.0%	1955	91.00%	1988	28.00%
1923	56.0%	1956	91.00%	1989	28.00%
1924	46.0%	1957	91.00%	1990	31.00%
1925	25.0%	1958	91.00%	1991	31.00%
1926	25.0%	1959	91.00%	1992	31.00%
1927	25.0%	1960	91.00%	1993	39.60%
1928	25.0%	1961	91.00%	1994	39.60%
1929	24.0%	1962	91.00%	1995	39.60%
1930	25.0%	1963	91.00%	1996	39.60%
1931	25.0%	1964	77.00%	1997	39.60%
1932	63.0%	1965	70.00%	1998	39.60%
1933	63.0%	1966	70.00%	1999	39.60%
1934	63.0%	1967	70.00%	2000	39.60%
1935	63.0%	1968	75.25%	2001	38.60%
1936	79.0%	1969	77.00%	2002	38.60%
1937	79.0%	1970	71.75%	2003	35.00%
1938	79.0%	1971	70.00%	2004	35.00%
1939	79.0%	1972	70.00%	2005	35.00%
1940	81.10%	1973	70.00%	2006	35.00%
1941	81.00%	1974	70.00%	2007	35.00%
1942	88.00%	1975	70.00%	2008	35.00%
1943	88.00%	1976	70.00%	2009	35.00%
1944	94.00%	1977	70.00%	2010	35.00%
1945	94.00%	1978	70.00%	2011	35.00%

Taxes down, market up

Great Depression

Stable Stock Market, prosperous Middle Class

Stock Market Rises Exponentially, Bubbles constantly inflate; burst

Note: This table contains a number of simplifications and ignores a number of factors, such as a maximum tax on earned income of 50 percent when the top rate was 70 percent and the current increase in rates due to income-related reductions in value of itemized deductions. Perhaps most importantly, it ignores the large increase in percentage of returns that were subject to this top rate.

Sources: Eugene Steuerle, The Urban Institute; Joseph Pechman, Federal Tax Policy; Joint Committee on Taxation, Summary of Conference Agreement on the Jobs and Growth Tax Relief Reconciliation Act of 2003, JCX-54-03, May 22, 2003; IRS Revised Tax Rate Schedules

Inverse Relationship between Rising Tax Rates and a Rising Stock Market

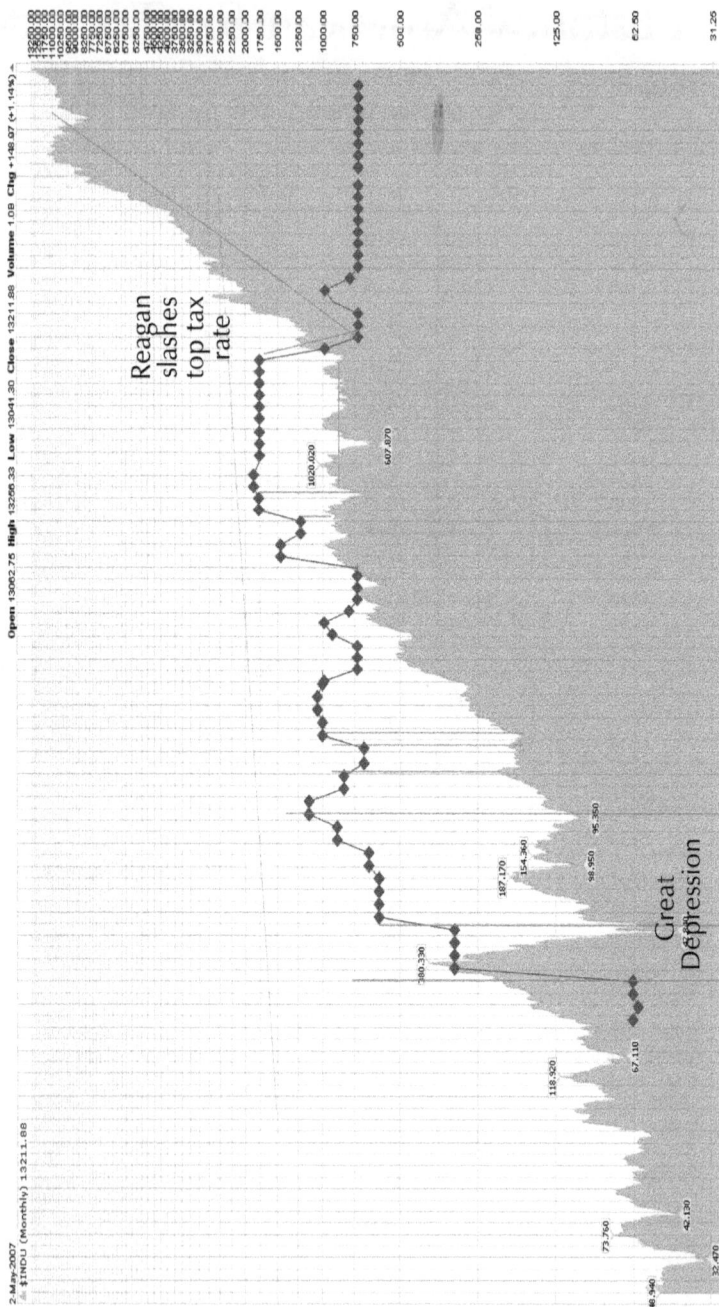

Reagan slashes top tax rate

Great Depression

A PEOPLE'S HISTORY OF CAPITALISM

What A Difference
A Dow Makes

A Logarithmic Dow, 1930-2010

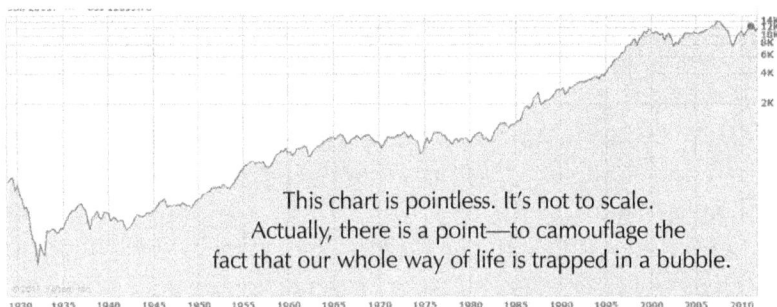

This chart is pointless. It's not to scale.
Actually, there is a point—to camouflage the
fact that our whole way of life is trapped in a bubble.

This is the chart of the Dow Jones Industrial Average we're all used to seeing. The Great Depression is that little blip over there on the far left. This is all smoke and mirrors, a drawing used by stock brokers to get you to buy into a retirement fund. So what's the trick? What's the con?

The con is that this Dow is not drawn to scale. It never says that anywhere. And this chart wasn't largely used prior to the 1980s when the bubble began.

A Linear Dow, 1930-2010

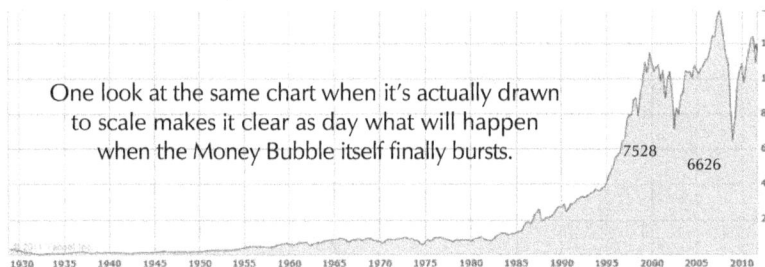

One look at the same chart when it's actually drawn
to scale makes it clear as day what will happen
when the Money Bubble itself finally bursts.

7528

6626

This is what the Dow Jones Industrial Average looks like when it's drawn to scale.

Now we can see the pattern emerging. It really starts to climb exponentially around 1985. That's when Reagan slashed corporate taxes from 70% to 28% in 8 years. We've been having boom and bust bubbles ever since.

When bubbles burst, they typically go back down exactly to the levels where they started inflating. One look at this chart and it's clear as day what happens when the Money Bubble itself bursts.

Creative Commons

WHAT?? No sources?

So this is the part of the appendix where you usually get sources and a bibliography and footnotes, oh my!

But why?

We've become a society obsessed with fact-checking and accuracy and credibility. We think that the inclusion of sources and bibliographies and footnotes lends credibility to every study, every fact, every survey. We can't just take people at their word! They need to tell us where they got that from! It's just not credible otherwise!

A laundry-list of sources indiscriminately provides an air of credibility. Truth, lies and videotape all have sources.

Yet when we see a laundry list of sources, extensive bibliographies and footnotes, doesn't that make us more inclined to take the author at his word, since he's gone through all the trouble of documenting his sources? These facts are well-researched! Look at this extensive list of sources!

We glance through the bibliography, but how often do most of us read the source books to decide for ourselves if an author's interpretations of the facts do justice to the so-called sources.

A laundry-list of sources does not discriminate. Providing sources provides an air of credibility to truth and lies alike. In fact, the sources for lies often far outnumber the sources for truth.

In being provided sources, we're actually encouraged to *just believe what we're told.*

◇

I'M NOT PROVIDING my sources because I *don't want you to take*

A PEOPLE'S HISTORY OF CAPITALISM

me at my word. Don't believe a word I say! Go do your homework. Go find out for yourself if what I'm telling you is right!

Don't be lulled into a false sense of confidence.

A book *supporting* global warming and Capitalism can be annotated and documented and footnoted ad nauseam ... the same as a book *bashing* global warming and Capitalism.

Some of us believe what Fox News tells us, and believe that tabloids check and double check and then check their facts again.

I'm sure tabloids and Fox News can provide as many sources (probably more) than I could.

Scientific studies performed at Harvard and Yale have to be confirmed by other studies at Princeton and so on. Then two months later a new study contradicts all the findings of the first.

◇

WHERE I'VE QUOTED individuals, I've attributed their words directly to them.

All of my other "sources" are licensed under the Creative Commons. That's the idea that knowledge is public, not proprietary. Knowledge is part of the commons, and it *should be* permitted to reproduce, distribute and disseminate knowledge without the express written consent of anyone.

The dissemination of knowledge should not be underwritten, patented or subjected to copyright law.

I have not used any sources from any books that are underwritten, patented or subject to copyright law.

I have found all of my information in the library of the creative commons. It really is a wonderful library.

You don't even need a library card.

Though you do have to know how to think for yourself.

Too many times, sources prevent us from doing just that.

(cc)

A Note About the Type...

ADBUSTERS magazine ran a campaign that said "Your average American can identify 1,000 corporate logos, and under 10 plant species."

I wondered how true that was.

Since one of our themes has been "Corporations Rule the World!" I thought it fitting to use corporate logo fonts to title various essays.

Logos aside, the most recognizable branding elements are fonts.

Mass marketing is one of the key weapons in the arsenal of Capitalism. And brand recognition is one of the key strategies.

So the 1,000 logos theory, I believe, extends beyond corporations. It extends to bands, art forms, literary works ... indeed any concept that has ever been subjected to the rigorous branding process of mass marketing.

The most widely-used font for logos is the simplest: Helvetica, or a variation thereof.

It surprised me to learn that the logos of so many brands were public domain. Just run of the mill fonts; Catull will forevermore remind us of Internet searches. Makes sense, really. Tap into the public domain, appropriate common, everyday things and let them do the work for you. Harness the power of people's already pre-conceived associations.

Commercials do it all the time. How many of your once-most-beloved rock songs is now infected with the taint of some Brand of Capitalism?

◇

MANY OF THE fonts used here are freely available for anyone to download in this wondrous land of the Internet we live in.

A PEOPLE'S HISTORY OF CAPITALISM

Others are available for a few bucks. In other cases, the fonts used here are not the exact fonts but artistic re-creations. Those are the most revealing. They bring to mind the brand they're associated with, even though they are not a precise carbon copy.

That's how pervasive these memes have become in our minds and in our media.

I wish I could imagine my consciousness free from all this flotsam floating around in there. Random, various jingles constantly getting stuck in my head and the like.

"Get out!" I scream to no avail. Sometimes it seems our voices cannot be heard over the pervasive din of Capitalism.